Best Practices for Training Early Childhood Professionals

SHARON BERGEN

Best Practices

for Training Early Childhood Professionals

Redleaf Press®
www.redleafpress.org
800-423-8309

Published by Redleaf Press
10 Yorkton Court
St. Paul, MN 55117
www.redleafpress.org

First edition 2009
Cover design by Brad Norr Design
Interior typeset in Sabon and Whitney and designed by Erin Kirk New
Developmental edit by Allison Fullenkamp
Printed in the United States of America
16   15   14   13   12   11   10   09   1   2   3   4   5   6   7   8

Redleaf Press Editorial, Design, and Production Staff
Editor-in-Chief: David Heath
Managing Editors: Laurie Herrmann and Douglas Schmitz
Acquisitions/Development Editor: Kyra Ostendorf
Creative Director: Jim Handrigan
Production Editor: Laura Maki
Production Assistant: Carla Valadez

Library of Congress Cataloging-in-Publication Data
Bergen, Sharon.
    Best practices for training early childhood professionals / Sharon
Bergen. — 1st ed.
       p. cm.
    Includes bibliographical references.
    ISBN 978-1-933653-40-2 (alk. paper)
   1. Early childhood teachers — In-service training. I. Title.
    LB1775.6.B465 2009
    370.71'5 — dc22   2008048485

Printed on acid-free paper

Best Practices for Training Early Childhood Professionals

Acknowledgments

The development of this book has been inspired by so many people that it is difficult to thank them all on this page. First, I want thank my always-inspiring family. Jamie, you, before anyone else, believed I could do this and waited patiently for many hours while I typed and typed. This is for you, above all. Next, there is the obvious inspiration—Allison, a most gentle and patient editor. Thank you for all your hard work in making this book better in so many ways. Finally, I want to thank David Heath and the entire Redleaf staff. Your encouragement and patience helped me to persevere, and your collaboration was essential to everything that shines in the final product.

Two other groups of people deserve thanks for their continuing inspiration. To all of the teachers, program directors, and trainers in the early childhood profession— you are a constant inspiration to me and to the families you serve. Thank you. Your work is rarely glamorous and often unrecognized, but always important.

And, finally, special thanks go to the Education and Training Department at Knowledge Learning Corporation. All of you hold special places in my heart; you are inspirations to me both personally and professionally. This book would not exist without your constant demonstration of everything that defines best practices. I never tire of learning from you.

Sharon Bergen

Introduction

Carol stared at the blank page. Tomorrow night she would conduct her monthly staff meeting and training session. She wondered aloud, "Why is it so hard to plan these meetings?" Mentally she reviewed the last few meetings, and each had been disappointing. Carol shook her head and thought, "I was a good teacher. Planning learning activities was one of my strengths. Why is planning for my teachers so challenging?"

Does this scene sound familiar? Across the early childhood profession, great teachers become program directors and suddenly become responsible for supervising adults and planning learning experiences for teachers rather than young children. If you are reading this book, you have either decided to become a trainer or, more likely, your job duties already include training. One of the interesting realities of the early childhood education profession is that the training of teachers is conducted by many individuals in a variety of capacities, few of whom have prepared professionally to work with adult learners.

Many of the skills that have helped you to be successful as a teacher or program director will also be useful in planning and delivering training sessions for your staff members. In fact, one of the goals of this book is to help you use the skills and knowledge you have developed as a teacher to plan and implement training for adults. You should see many parallels between what you already know about early childhood education and the skills and concepts you will use to train teachers.

Throughout the text, the term *teacher* is used to refer to staff members of all levels in the program. The term *director* is used to refer to the person responsible for planning the program's training and staff development.

Although there are certainly men in the field, the overwhelming majority of early childhood teachers and directors are women. Throughout the book, the pronouns *she*, *her*, and *hers* are used to avoid the more awkward *he or she*, *him or her*, and *his or hers* usages. There was no intent to ignore or diminish the positive role male teachers and directors play in early childhood settings.

The first section of this book describes a framework to organize your thinking about training. This framework uses what you already know about developmentally appropriate practices for working with young learners. In this section, we will also look at the role and goals of training within early childhood programs.

The second section of the book is intended to help you understand the task of working with adult learners. Like children, adults have some characteristics as learners that we can expect and plan for as we design training sessions. Teachers also progress through stages of development as they gain professional experience and tenure in the field. Understanding these stages helps you plan learning activities to best meet the needs of the adults with whom you work.

The final section of the book provides a methodology for designing training experiences and tips and techniques for implementing training activities. Mastering these methods will help you use your planning time wisely and will increase your comfort and confidence as a trainer. These best practices are used by trainers in a wide variety of professions and are used by many early childhood training programs to develop

employees and to create high-quality programs.

Throughout all of the sections of the book, you will find activities and exercises to enhance both your training skills and the organization of your center's training plan. These activities and exercises are designed to help you to employ the best practices described in the book and to develop and implement an overarching training plan in your program. In the early childhood classroom, we use a curriculum and lesson plans to guide our teaching and ensure that the children in our care receive a well-rounded early education. Similarly, directors or trainers should develop a plan for training to ensure that teachers receive well-rounded professional development. The information, tools, and examples included in these pages can be used to support your continuing development as a trainer and to begin your work in developing specific plans for the training programs you administer and the professionals you serve.

A Note about the Audience for this Book

In most early childhood programs, directors are responsible for the planning and implementation of staff training and professional development. Therefore, this book was written with program directors in mind. At the same time, assistant directors, trainers, and others who support the training of teachers will find this information equally helpful.

SECTION 1

Establishing a Framework

CHAPTER 1

The Role of Training in Teacher Development and Program Quality

Fran stared at the agenda for her Super Saturday teacher training day:

- *thirty minutes for welcome and introduction of new teachers*
- *two hours to introduce the new assessment tool*
- *one hour for lunch*
- *two hours to renew the first aid training*

Fran worried. Only two hours were left to teach everything else her teachers needed to know, and she wasn't sure where to start. "I guess I'll focus on discipline—they always ask for that topic."

Every year, early childhood programs devote valuable time and resources to teacher training. You have probably planned and implemented a variety of teacher training experiences already—some were great while others were disappointing.

All too often, training plans are developed with one goal in mind—fitting the most-requested topics into the number of hours required or available for professional development.

If you are reading this book, you probably have an interest in improving the results of your training and in capitalizing on the investment you are making in the teachers' professional development. Perhaps you would like your training efforts to do more for your program than merely meet regulatory requirements or fill up the time allocated for training at teacher meetings and other functions. Fortunately, a number of best practices exist that can help you to improve the effectiveness of your training efforts. Most of the changes you can make will not increase the expense of the training you are offering, yet they will make the investment more worthwhile and effective.

In this chapter, we will look at a simple definition of training, your role as a trainer,

5

and some of the reasons for conducting training programs. This foundational information will set the stage for the development of your training plans and the evaluation of your training efforts.

A Definition of *Training*

Many terms associated with the development of employees are used interchangeably—for example, many people use the term *professional development* instead of the term *training*. Or you may see terms such as *in-service training* and *pre-service training* used to describe various teacher training requirements. Unfortunately, a wide variety of terms are used with little consistency throughout the early childhood literature and across varying agencies and regulatory bodies. As a trainer for your program, you must familiarize yourself with the terms used by your program and the regulatory agencies in your area. Familiarizing yourself with terms enhances your credibility and helps eliminate confusion for you and your trainees.

In general, *professional development* refers to a broad category of activities and includes training, credit-based coursework, mentoring, and other activities designed to support professional growth. For example, a teacher might attend a specific conference or volunteer as a participant in a professional task force as part of his professional development. *Training* is a more specific

term that is used to describe an activity designed to improve employee knowledge, skills, or attitudes and to change behavior on the job. A teacher might attend a training session designed to introduce a new preschool curriculum and then implement that curriculum in her classroom. Remember that training always has the ultimate goal of changing behavior to improve job performance. Therefore, training has a practical application and a link to the participant's job expectations.

When we think of training, we usually picture a classroom with an instructor (or trainer) leading a group of participants (or trainees). While instructor-led or facilitated training is certainly one method of training, there are many others. Trainers, like teachers of young children, use a variety of methods to meet the learning needs of their trainees. Training might take any of the following forms:

- individual coaching or mentoring
- self-study using print or electronic media
- action learning, study groups, or communities of practice
- on-the-job training, including demonstrations, shadowing, and guided practice
- online (Web-based) training or distance education
- computer-based training

These training methods, along with the many forms of instructor-led experiences, are appropriate solutions for differing

Spotlight on ASTD

The American Society for Training and Development (ASTD) has researched and described the competencies and practices associated with training excellence. Its Web site, conferences, publications, and certification programs are excellent sources of information and professional development for anyone choosing a career path as a trainer. Trainers from a wide variety of professions participate in ASTD. Many also choose to pursue certification to enhance their credibility and professionalism. For more information about the organization, local affiliates, conferences, or certification courses, see the ASTD Web site: www.astd.org.

training needs. The challenge is matching the right teaching or training method to the learning need—as you do when teaching young children.

Regardless of the training methods used, many regulatory agencies differentiate between pre-service training and in-service training. Typically, *pre-service training* refers to education or training requirements that must be completed to qualify to work in a specific capacity. For example, a state may require twelve hours of pre-service training in early childhood education to qualify as an assistant teacher. *In-service training* refers to training that is completed while holding a particular position. A state may require a certain number of hours of in-service training for teachers employed in child care programs. These requirements vary from state to state and

many even vary within states, based on the licensing agencies involved. Often, in-service training is measured by the number of hours per year each employee must complete. Trainees expect you as the trainer to be knowledgeable about training requirements, so it is important to be aware of the pre-service and in-service requirements of the regulatory agencies that govern your program.

In addition to knowing the training requirements, it is essential for you to understand the theories and professional guidelines associated with training. Training has its own set of professional guidelines, associations, theorists, and well-known and respected practitioners (again, just like early childhood education). To be successful as a trainer, you need to combine your knowledge of early childhood education content with the principles and methods used in expert training practices for adult learners.

The Many Reasons to Conduct Training

The purpose of a training session guides its development and the methods used to implement the training. You may conduct training for any of the following reasons:

- to comply with regulatory requirements
- to change teacher behavior
- to implement new policies, programs, or teaching methods
- to change attitudes
- to develop teamwork and build a sense of community among teachers
- to improve program quality

Comply with Regulatory Requirements

Most programs have some requirements for orientation training or for annual training of employees. For example, your state may require three hours of training on a variety of health and safety topics for each new teacher.

Change Teacher Behavior

One of the most universal purposes of training is to change on-the-job behavior, usually to improve practices or to enhance the quality of the program. For example, you may conduct a training session designed to increase the quantity and quality of teacher-child interactions during outdoor play.

Implement New Policies, Programs, or Teaching Methods

The way we do things in early childhood programs changes regularly. Because research continually informs our practice and often sparks the use of new teaching techniques or program ideas, trainings that support change are continually needed. For example, if your program is changing its curriculum to reflect a project approach, you might conduct a training to introduce this method to the teachers. When your program changes its procedures, another training is usually involved.

Change Attitudes

How teachers think about their practice is as important as their skills and knowledge base. Common sense tells us that teachers are more likely to implement practices they believe are effective and avoid those practices they do not believe in. Research consistently shows that teachers' beliefs about practices influence what they do in the classroom (National Research Council 2001, 264–265). Sometimes training is used to influence teachers' beliefs and attitudes in favor of particular methods or practices. Imagine that you are planning to implement a series of training sessions to introduce elements of language and culture among the families who participate in your program.

The goal of these sessions may extend beyond providing information to promoting openness between teachers and families and appreciation for other cultures. Your real goal may be to change attitudes as well as behaviors.

Develop Teamwork and Build a Sense of Community among Teachers

Teachers rarely work in isolation. Even teachers who work individually in a classroom depend upon others in the program to meet the complex and challenging needs of the children they provide care for. Teamwork is an essential component of quality early childhood environments. Therefore, it is logical to expect that some portion of the program's overall training plan would be devoted to building teamwork among its teachers. To illustrate this idea, suppose you are planning a training session about parent communication and teachers' roles in parent events. During this training session, you might introduce information about interactions with families or reinforce the program's principles for customer service. You might also conduct activities to build the kind of communication and team spirit among your participants that would be necessary to plan and implement a program-sponsored event.

Improve Program Quality

A great deal of research points toward the belief that training can influence program quality directly and indirectly. This topic will be explored in greater detail later in this chapter.

Keep in mind that the underlying reasons for training are not mutually exclusive. A training session may touch on several of the reasons listed on page 8. For example, a training session might begin with an ice-breaking activity that promotes teamwork and include information and activities designed to build skills and influence teachers' attitudes. At the same time, this session might also fulfill a regulatory requirement for training hours for those participating.

Training Priorities: A Delicate Balance

Despite the many reasons to conduct training, most early childhood programs cannot realistically provide all of the training desired because of budget and time constraints. Even if it were possible to provide unlimited training opportunities, trainers must work to balance training priorities with program needs. Teachers working with young children conduct a similar balancing act. When they plan a curriculum, teachers balance planning for children's individual needs with their need to be ready for school, to learn about certain subjects and content, and to flourish in social situations. Later in this chapter, we will explore two of the training priorities you will address as part of your overall program training plan, starting with compliance training and moving on to program goals. In chapter 4, we will discuss the third area of training priorities: individual teacher training. Before we consider each of the priorities that will shape the content of your training, we must consider the importance of planning.

Developing Training Plans for the Program

Most teachers use a curriculum and lesson plans to guide their teaching. These tools help teachers cover a broad range of content and make the most of learning opportunities in the classroom. Similarly, trainers create plans to ensure that they have identified the goals of their training program and to support effective, high-quality implementation of that information. Before you begin crafting training activities, you should identify the priorities and goals you have for your training.

As a trainer, you are constantly balancing the three priorities of your program's training plan: compliance training, goal support, and individual needs. First, you must provide for required compliance training. Although you may not present all of this training yourself, you must include it in your overall plan. Second, you must plan for training that is needed to support your program goals. This might include training on a new curriculum you are introducing or training to address weaknesses in your

program's quality. Finally, you must plan for the training needs of individual teachers. This part of your training plan involves creating individual professional development plans for each of the teachers you support.

Throughout this book, you will complete activities to help you build a training plan. Completing each form as it is introduced will lead you through the process needed to develop a well-rounded, step-by-step training plan. If you serve more than one program, you can use the blank forms in the appendix on page 147 to develop additional planning documents.

Compliance Training Requirements

Early childhood programs are highly regulated by a number of agencies. For example, Head Start programs are part of a federally sponsored program and are required to meet the standards of the national Head Start governance agencies as well as the regulations of local child care licensing agencies and the local health department. As a trainer, you must understand the regulations and training requirements that affect the programs you work with. Always remember that you may need to meet requirements from a number of federal, state, and local agencies.

The sample form that follows will help identify and document the compliance training that must be part of your program's

Training Plan: Compliance Training

∙∙

Program name _____

What agencies govern the program? _____

_____

_____

What other programs, such as accreditation, quality rating systems, or special funding sources, affect the training requirements?

PROGRAM	IMPACT

Briefly list some of the training requirements with which the program must comply.

New employee orientation _____

_____

Annual training requirements _____

_____

Special topics (first aid, CPR, blood-borne pathogens, child abuse detection and reporting, shaken baby syndrome, food handling, medication administration). List each topic and the training requirements.

TOPIC	TRAINING REQUIREMENTS

training plan. Use licensing regulations, accreditation standards, and other program regulations to help answer each question and develop a complete inventory of the training priorities imposed by various agencies and accrediting bodies. For a reproducible copy of Training Plan: Compliance Training, see form 1 in the appendix.

Training to Meet Program Goals and Enhance Quality

Think about the goals you have for your program that may need to be supported by your training plans. Consider your program's mission and any plans you have for program changes or growth. These are helpful starting points for your plans. Not every goal you have for your program affects your training plans. As you think about your goals, ask yourself, "What training do teachers need to reach this goal?"

Developing Goals

Writing goals can be a tricky task. Goals can quickly become a list of to-do items that never quite get done. Using a tool known as the SMART formula will help you clarify your goals and create a deadline for achieving each goal (Loo 2006). SMART goals are Specific, Measurable, Attainable, Relevant, and Time sensitive; you describe each goal in a statement including each of these characteristics.

Ask yourself the following questions to SMART-test each goal:

Specific	Is it clear what is to be accomplished?
Measurable	Will you be able to measure whether the goal has been accomplished?
Attainable	Is this goal realistic for this program? Will the program be able to accomplish this goal with effort and focus?
Relevant	Does this goal match the needs of this program? Will accomplishing this goal energize employees?
Time sensitive	Is there a clear time line for accomplishing this goal? (While it is sometimes hard to commit to a deadline, picking a date for achieving a goal greatly increases the likelihood that you will do so.)

Consider the following goal: to use teacher training on literacy programs to support obtaining three stars in the state quality-rating system by the end of this year. This goal meets the SMART criteria because it identifies a specific goal (obtaining three stars in the quality-rating system). Presumably this goal is attainable for the program and is relevant to its success. The goal is measurable, and it identifies a specific time frame.

You can use the form on the following page to practice using the SMART formula to write program goals that will affect your training plan. Remember, goals are important because you need to know what your training must accomplish so you can prioritize your efforts and plan for all of the training that teachers will need. For a reproducible copy of Training Plan: Program Goals, see form 2 in the appendix.

Training and Program Quality: A Special Relationship

Keesha felt lucky to be involved in a project to help her program achieve accreditation. The specialist who visited the program had been very encouraging about the program's chances of achieving accreditation. Then Keesha reviewed the list of program improvements the specialist left on her desk. She realized that although the visit went well, she certainly had some work to do before the next visit. Optimistically, Keesha told the assistant director, "Looks like we'll have plenty to cover at our next training day!"

Many of your training goals are probably related to improving or maintaining the quality of your program. In early childhood education, we often have used training to improve program quality and to guarantee satisfactory services for the families enrolled in our programs. The belief that training supports quality has a long history in our profession and is, in most cases, well supported by our professional research (Tout, Zaslow, and Berry 2006, 91–92). This is such a common practice that you already may be using training as a means to improve quality within your programs.

The link between training and quality exists for a number of reasons. First, teachers with enhanced knowledge and skills perform better in the classroom and therefore provide a higher-quality program. This commonsense argument is based on the belief that teachers do, in fact, learn new knowledge and skills in training and that afterward they apply their new knowledge and skill set in the classroom. While this is not always the case, as we will explore later in the book, quite often this is what occurs.

Second, the link between training and quality is reinforced by the expectations of our regulatory agencies and accrediting bodies. In many states and among many agencies, training is required to support program quality, and teachers are required to participate in training prior to and during their tenure in early education programs. These requirements are based on the research that describes the impact of training on the care that children receive and the services teachers provide.

Third, early childhood research supports the link between training and program quality. The highly regarded *Eager to Learn* report summarizes the literature on education and training of the early

Training Plan: Program Goals

· ·

Program name _____

Use the space below to draft two or three program goals that will affect your training plans in the next two or three months.

1. _____

_____

_____

_____

_____

2. _____

_____

_____

_____

_____

3. _____

_____

_____

_____

_____

Now, review each goal. Does it fit the SMART formula—is it Specific, Measurable, Attainable, Relevant, and Time sensitive? If not, revise your goals to incorporate each of these elements.

childhood workforce (National Research Council 2001, 270–276). Among other conclusions, this summary demonstrates that well-designed training programs can and do positively influence teachers' skills in supporting literacy and math development, providing sensitive care, adhering to principles of developmentally appropriate practice, and enhancing the overall quality of program environments.

At the same time, we can all think of programs that provide a great deal of training but do not reach high levels of quality. How can this happen? Despite all of the evidence supporting the positive influence of training on program quality, the case for training is still inconclusive for a number of reasons. First, while much of the research provides evidence of the effectiveness of training on overall program quality, less evidence supports the effect on outcomes for children. Many studies rely on the assumption that improving the program quality naturally results in improved outcomes for the children who participate in the program (Fukkink and Lont 2007, 294–311). While it seems logical that a quality program will have a positive effect on the children who participate, child outcomes are influenced by other factors that cannot be improved by training, such as the children's home environment or health.

Second, training, while valuable, is not the cure-all for program quality because it does not affect all of the processes and structural elements in programs that influence overall quality. For example, training may positively influence a teacher's behavior, but it does not change the materials a teacher has access to—and available materials can directly affect the breadth and depth of a program for any teacher, no matter how well trained.

Finally, the influence that training can have on program quality is limited by the design and implementation of the training. While the research supports the positive potential of well-designed and expertly implemented training, it also notes that much of the pre-service and in-service training in which teachers participate is uneven in quality, often isolated from program goals, and frequently ineffective in influencing teaching practices (Maxwell, Feild, and Clifford 2006, 21–48). Think back over your own experiences as a trainee: you may be able to recall a number of training experiences that failed to advance your teaching skills or your professional knowledge.

While the inconclusive nature of the early childhood research on teacher training might appear discouraging, it actually is very consistent with the beliefs that pervade the training profession. Throughout the training profession, regardless of the industry it serves, researchers, experts, and well-known practitioners emphasize the limitations of training and its impact on employee behavior and argue against the notion that training is the solution to all performance problems (Brinkerhoff 2006, 12).

Training Challenges and Misconceptions

Training can have a powerful affect on employee behavior and on the quality of a program. At the same time, we should be cautious about overstating the potential impact training can have on teacher behavior, program quality, or child outcomes. In the 1970s, Thomas Gilbert, a performance engineer, developed an approach to understanding employee performance that he called the behavior engineering model (Gilbert 2007, 88). While still widely used and acknowledged today, Gilbert's succinct way of characterizing the influences on employee behavior sparked a new way of thinking among trainers and human resource professionals.

Gilbert's model simply declares that employees are influenced by a range of environmental and individual factors including the availability of information, resources, and incentives, as well as the their own knowledge, capacity, and motives. Gilbert's work is important to all trainers because it supports our understanding of training's potential and limitations. The following principles are based on the work of Thomas Gilbert and his successors.

Training Addresses Employees' Lack of Knowledge or Skills

Resist the temptation to use training as the remedy for every employee challenge. Although teachers may fail to perform as expected for a variety of reasons—for example, lack of resources, low motivation, and little incentive for excellence—training is best utilized when poor performance is the result of absence of knowledge or skills. For example, training is helpful when implementing new programs, procedures, or policies because teachers probably lack knowledge about these new developments. On the other hand, if a teacher knows how to implement a new procedure involving, say, administering medication, but lacks the equipment to do so, all of the training in the world won't change her ability to administer medication in the way you have demonstrated during training.

Training Alone Is Rarely Effective in Changing Behavior

It makes sense that it takes more than training to really change employee behavior. Recall the teacher mentioned in the previous example who has received training in implementing a new medication administration procedure. What would happen if, along with the training, the teacher administering medicine also received the necessary forms and supplies as well as encouragement and support from her director during the early days of using the new procedure? As you can imagine, this combination of training, resources, and manager support would greatly increase the likelihood that she would try and continue to use the new procedure in the classroom—a permanent change in behavior.

All Training Is not the Same

Like all instruction, training should conform to principles of instructional design and use what we know about effective adult learning. Good training involves much more than simply showing a trainee a new skill or explaining a new concept. If changing behavior were as easy as seeing the skill done well, then everyone who has watched championship golf on television would be an excellent golfer! The chapters that follow will introduce you to many of the principles and practices that guide effective training practices. Implementing these ideas in your training sessions will help you increase the chances of your trainees learning and applying the information.

Training Is the Means to an End, not the Goal

Those of us who enjoy training and believe in its effectiveness also need to remind ourselves regularly that the true goal of our work is to improve the on-the-job performance of our trainees. No matter how creative, enjoyable, or well-liked a training session might be, it is only truly effective if the trainees use the knowledge, skills, or attitudes developed in the training to advance classroom quality, enhance child outcomes, or otherwise improve their teaching performance. Keeping this principle in mind helps trainers resist the temptation to use training gimmicks, games, or other methods that are not supported by the training session's instructional goals or objectives.

Before we move on to consider the principles that surround the design and development of training, it is important to consider your role as a trainer. Although a complete review of trainer development and competence is beyond the scope of this book, a short introduction to your role may help you make the best use of the best practices shared throughout the remainder of the chapters.

Becoming a Trainer: Opportunities and Responsibilities

Pilar looked across the group of participants in the conference room. Then she looked up at the trainer in the front of the room. To herself she whispered, "I sure wish I were standing up there instead of sitting here." Pilar wondered what it would take to become a trainer and influence so many teachers.

Much of the responsibility for the success of your training programs and sessions rests with you. You have a significant opportunity to use training to improve quality in early childhood programs and to enhance the experiences of children and families. At the same time, assuming training responsibilities also means that you must focus on an additional set of professional principles, skills, and obligations. In your capacity as the supervisor of teachers, the subject matter expert, or the training professional in a program, you will find opportunities to strengthen and use your training knowledge and skills.

Director as Trainer

In early childhood education, directors are often the head trainers for the teachers in their program. This is true for a number of reasons. First, if you are a supervisor of teachers, you are in a unique position to understand the development needs of your teachers. When you conduct classroom observations or otherwise interact with teachers, you are able to gather information about their challenges and successes. This information will help you select training topics to support their developing knowledge and skills.

Second, as a director, you are often the person responsible for setting the program goals requiring training support. For example, you may be the one who chooses to implement a new policy or procedure that will require training to get started. In this role, you must look beyond the needs of individual teachers and consider the needs of the entire program and the families it serves. Some of the training needs you identify in this area will come from the mission of your program; others will come from your goals for growing and improving your program.

Third, you probably enjoy teaching others and find the time you spend supporting teacher development worthwhile and personally fulfilling. Many directors,

especially those who began their careers as teachers, find a great deal of satisfaction in continuing their teaching role through teacher training. Although adult learners are different from young children, much of the satisfaction you derive from helping others learn new skills can be found in your role as a teacher trainer.

Finally, in many programs, it is financially impractical to hire a person to conduct all of the training for teachers or to send teachers to training sessions outside the program. Even in programs with dedicated positions for trainers, directors often conduct part of the overall training plan.

Subject Matter Expert

Trainers often begin their careers as subject matter experts or supervisors and later develop and hone their training abilities. For example, the trainer at a bank probably started in one of the jobs he now trains others to perform. Stretching your skills as a supervisor and a subject matter expert is one of the opportunities that training presents for you as a program director.

Supervisors generally have some training responsibilities as part of their job descriptions. In coaching and mentoring the teachers who report to you, you are already doing some of the work associated with training. Still, not everyone who supervises others or has training responsibilities is equally skilled at conducting training activities or events. Perhaps you

Spotlight on Training Registry

In some states or for programs under some auspices, training may need to be conducted by a registered or approved trainer. In these instances, trainers are often required to have specific credentials or participate in train-the-trainer programs to develop training skills and to ensure consistently high quality of training development and delivery. Check your local regulations to understand any requirements for hiring registered or approved trainers for your program.

have participated in a training session with a trainer who was extremely knowledgeable and a true expert in subject matter, but she was not a very engaging trainer. This experience illustrates the often-overlooked obstacle that knowledge about a topic does not guarantee excellence as a trainer.

Training Expertise

If you have already conducted training sessions with individuals or groups of teachers. you may have some ideas about your talents and your opportunities for improvement as a trainer. The American Society for Training and Development (ASTD) has a well-developed and comprehensive list of trainer competencies. Let's examine some of the basic attributes you will need to be successful as a trainer. Consider how well each of the following phrases describes you:

☐ assertive in group situations
☐ comfortable as the speaker in front of groups of varying sizes
☐ confident in presenting ideas
☐ able to address conflict and disagreement
☐ organized in developing learning experiences and planning training events
☐ comfortable creating and using a variety of audiovisual aids, including computer-based applications
☐ flexible and able to adapt plans in progress
☐ verbally articulate and able to speak professionally in scripted and unscripted situations
☐ enthusiastic and engaging, able to make the learning experiences fun
☐ open to change and embracing of innovation and improvement
☐ interested in research and learning about and trying new things—a lifelong learner

☐ willing to be scrutinized as a role model

☐ genuinely concerned about the learning of others

In addition to these personal attributes, trainers need adequate subject matter knowledge and skills in designing and implementing training for adults. Most trainers develop these with time, study, and practice. Crafting your own professional development plan to enhance your knowledge and skills as a trainer is an important step toward success.

Use the Trainer Self-Assessment on the following page to understand the knowledge and skills you now possess and some of your opportunities for development. Complete the assessment and use it to begin your professional development plan. For a reproducible copy of Trainer Self-Assessment, see form 3 in the appendix.

Summary

Training can be a powerful ally for any program director and an effective means to enhance teacher performance and program quality. Very few programs have no training requirements, and even if that were the case, wise directors would continue to use effective, well-designed training to get the most from their teachers.

So far we have looked at the definition of *training* and considered some of the reasons why you might implement training in your program. We also have reviewed some of the personal attributes needed in a trainer and have identified some opportunities to enhance your skills.

Trainer Self-Assessment

· ·

Name _____   Date _____

Check the box that best describes your abilities and attributes at this time.

PERSONAL ATTRIBUTES	Not at all	Somewhat	Mostly	Always
I am considered an effective communicator.				
I respect confidences and personal information.				
I am able to be fair in handling conflicts and disputes.				
I convey respect for others, including those with different perspectives from my own.				
I enjoy learning new things.				
I usually consider change to be positive.				
I am flexible and can adapt quickly to changing circumstances.				
SUBJECT MATTER KNOWLEDGE				
People often seek my input on concerns or problems related to the program.				
I regularly attend trainings or otherwise update my knowledge about early childhood education.				
I value diverse points of view about program goals, procedures, and outcomes.				
TRAINING METHODS				
I am comfortable in front of others.				
I can present information forcefully and clearly.				
I am a good listener.				
Others find me motivating.				
I am able to recognize anxiety or discomfort in others.				
I know and can use a wide variety of training techniques.				
I am interested in what others think and say about my training abilities.				
STRATEGY AND LEADERSHIP				
I am able to link program concerns or goals to training solutions.				
I am able to prioritize the needs of teachers.				
I often am selected to lead groups or projects.				
I am aware of a wide variety of resources available in my community.				

List each item to which you responded "not at all" or "somewhat." These are your areas to concentrate on when creating your professional development plan.

CHAPTER 2

A Framework for Organizing Knowledge about Training

Leisha stared at her accreditation paperwork. How could she ever create a professional development plan for her center when every teacher seemed to need something a bit different? She thought, "When I was a teacher, we all went to the same training session every month. That simple plan worked for us; we did fine. Why does this have to be so complicated now?"

In addition to planning training activities that meet the compliance needs of your program and help advance your program goals, you will need to plan for the individual needs of the teachers you support. Organizing what you know about the developmental needs of teachers can appear to be a daunting task. Early childhood teachers struggle with an equally challenging task when they think about the individual needs of the children in their classrooms. Teachers must balance what they know about children's development,

the demands of school readiness and parent preferences, and program goals to construct classroom curriculum and activities that are effective and worthwhile. Your task as the trainer for your program is similar. In many respects, your role as a trainer could be described as the lead teacher in your program's adult learning classroom. Thinking about your role in this way will help you use much of what you know about good teaching to create high-quality training experiences for your teachers.

Using Models to Understand Practice

Mental models, or visuals, help us organize and remember information. Adults naturally create mental models of information to assist in organizing and remembering the information they encounter (Clark and Lyons 2004, 22–24). For example, when you read the ingredients for a recipe, you

Three Dimensions of Knowledge

Knowledge of
Age and Stage
Characteristics

Knowledge of
Individual
Characteristics

Knowledge of
the Social and Cultural
Contexts

may quite naturally imagine each ingredient on a shopping list. By doing so, you can then recall your shopping list when you gather the ingredients to begin cooking.

Many texts, job aids, and training sessions use mental models to organize information and to enhance memory. In the chapters that follow, we will use a simple mental model based on three dimensions of knowledge introduced in the National Association for the Education of Young Children's (NAEYC) developmentally appropriate practice guidelines (Bredekamp and Copple 1997, 9).

These building blocks will help you visualize the pieces of knowledge on which you will build your program's training plan. Each area will be briefly described in the sections that follow and will be covered more thoroughly in subsequent chapters.

The Developmentally Appropriate Practice Model

Since their original publication more than twenty years ago, NAEYC's guidelines for developmentally appropriate practice, or DAP, have supported and influenced early childhood education. Teacher preparation courses, training sessions, and a wide variety of other programs refer to and support the understanding of developmentally appropriate practice. While elements of DAP are often misunderstood or misapplied, the guidelines and principles as a whole are well-known and embraced throughout the profession.

The Three Dimensions of Knowledge Fit Adult Learning

As you will see in the following sections and subsequent chapters, the DAP framework is broad enough to fit easily

Three Dimensions of Knowledge

Knowledge of Age and Stage Characteristics	
Knowledge of Individual Characteristics	Knowledge of the Social and Cultural Contexts

around many of the adult learning principles that guide good training practice.

Using a Familiar Framework Increases Your Confidence

Based on the belief that you already have some familiarity with DAP and its principles and guidelines, this framework is a natural starting place to add new dimensions to your knowledge. One of the goals of this book is to help you *apply what you already know* in new ways. Using a familiar framework supports that goal and increases the chance that you will be able to apply new ideas in your own training practice.

The Three Dimensions of Knowledge

In their well-regarded work *Developmentally Appropriate Practice in Early*

Childhood Programs, Bredekamp and Copple (1997) describe the three dimensions of knowledge that inform early childhood education. These are knowledge of typical age and stage development, individual characteristics, and the social and cultural contexts. They also observe, "The concept of developmentally appropriate practice is not limited in applicability to young children but can be applied throughout the life span" (36). It is in the spirit of their research that we apply the three dimensions of knowledge to our understanding of the needs of teachers in our training work.

Knowledge of Age- and Stage-Related Characteristics

Human development occurs in a relatively orderly and predictable way. In much the same way that we can predict what a

Three Dimensions of Knowledge

```
┌─────────────────────────┐
│    Knowledge of         │
│    Age and Stage        │
│    Characteristics      │
│                         │
├──────────────────┬──────┴──────────────────┐
│   Knowledge of   │    Knowledge of         │
│   Individual     │    the Social and       │
│   Characteristics│    Cultural             │
│                  │    Contexts             │
└──────────────────┴─────────────────────────┘
```

typically developing preschooler is able to do and might be interested in, we can make some similar predictions about adults of different ages. For example, we can assume that most twenty-somethings are in their early years in the professional world. They have had limited job experience and may still be learning about workplace expectations and behavior. We can expect that more experienced adults will bring a greater number and variety of experiences and younger, less experienced adults will bring fewer work-related experiences. Regardless of the number of experiences adults possess, we know that these experiences shape the ways in which they learn and how they apply the information offered in training sessions.

Much is also known about how teachers develop throughout their professional lives. Those who are new to teaching have different concerns and training needs than experienced teachers. Understanding the stages of teacher development can help you as a trainer to predict the needs your trainees may have at differing points in their careers.

Knowledge of Individual Characteristics, such as Strengths, Interests, and Needs

Although human development remains fairly predictable across the life span, like children, adults of differing ages do not have the same strengths, interests, and needs. In fact, individual variation may be more visible among adults of the same age than among children because adults have had a greater number of life experiences to influence their development and expose them to new interests (Knowles 1980, 49–58).

Natural abilities and challenges contribute to adults' temperaments and personalities. You may know adults who are naturally

Three Dimensions of Knowledge

Knowledge of Age and Stage Characteristics	
Knowledge of Individual Characteristics	Knowledge of the Social and Cultural Contexts

adventurous and others who are reluctant to try new things. Their education and life experiences affect the knowledge and skills they bring to the workplace (Taylor, Marienau, and Fiddler 2000, 4–9). You may have some teachers in your program with advanced degrees in early childhood education and others with a high school diploma and years of informal experiences through parenting or caring for the children of others. The diverse experiences of teachers, along with their wide range of interests and preferences, will help determine their training needs and influence the ways in which they are likely to respond to training activities.

Knowledge of the Social and Cultural Contexts

Adults often reflect their social and cultural milieus. Ideally, the teachers in any program represent a broad range of cultural heritages. This diversity among teachers

strengthens the program, but it also presents a challenge for you as a trainer. How adults participate in and respond to learning experiences is influenced by language and culture, just as it is for children.

Other considerations influencing adult learners are the social and cultural contexts of the program in which they work. Every early childhood program is somewhat different. Even programs with the same ownership or those operating under the same leadership are not entirely identical in environment, atmosphere, or the ways in which work is organized and accomplished. Think for a minute about a program familiar to you. It has its own traditions and ways of doing things. Some of these practices are a result of rules and regulations; others are a result of habits that have accumulated over the years the program has operated. These formal and informal routines and behaviors

Three Dimensions of Knowledge

Knowledge of Age and Stage Characteristics	
Knowledge of Individual Characteristics	Knowledge of the Social and Cultural Contexts

comprise the culture of your center's program (Albrecht 2002, 37).

Adult Learning Theory

We know much about the characteristics of teachers working in early childhood education. Research indicates that over 2 million individuals work in paid positions as teachers of young children (Kagan, Kauerz, and Tarrant 2008, 23–25). These teachers work in a wide variety of programs, including home-based care, center-based care, Head Start, and school district-sponsored early childhood classrooms. While it is fair to say that the early childhood workforce represents the diverse nature of our country, research indicates that there are two predictable similarities among teachers in early education programs. First, most teachers

in early childhood programs are female—about 95 percent of the workforce (Kagan, Kauerz, and Tarrant 2008, 23–25). Second, early childhood teachers are more likely to have less formal education than teachers in elementary or secondary programs. Nevertheless, a broad range of educational backgrounds, such as education level and teaching experience, can be found among early childhood teachers in any program (Brandon and Martinez-Beck 2006, 63–66). Within any program you may find teachers with no college education as well as teachers with bachelor's and master's degrees.

Naturally, teachers in early education programs mirror the range of interests, capacities, and motivations found among other adults. Although all of the adults teaching in the program have chosen a teaching profession and have chosen to work with young children, they may not be similarly motivated or approach their learning and professional development in exactly the same manner. As a trainer, you are likely to encounter adult learners who share some similarities yet differ in many important ways.

At this point, you may be thinking back to your own training as a teacher of young children. You learned that young children share some similar characteristics but are also unique in many ways. You probably studied theorists, such as Piaget, Vygotsky, and Erikson, who helped explain what you could expect from children at differing stages of development. Luckily, a rich body of research about adult learners can help guide you. Understanding some of the theoretical underpinning of adult learning explained in the following sections will help you understand the age- and stage-related characteristics of adults. Doing so will make you more effective as a trainer.

Adult Learning Theorists

Like childhood, adulthood has its own significant body of research, researchers, and practitioners devoted to expanding current knowledge and applying that knowledge to the field. While each theorist has an important point of view on adult learning, theorists agree on the fact that adults and children learn differently in a number of important ways.

Many theorists who have researched and written about the development of children have also been interested in adult development or development across the entire life span. Although a complete description of each of the major theories of adult development and learning is beyond the scope of this book, a brief overview of some of the best-known adult learning theorists is included here.

Like new research in child development, the body of knowledge on adult learning and best practices for training adults is constantly growing. Adult learning theorists and researchers are not always in complete agreement about the best approaches and strategies. What is most commonly agreed upon is Knowles' andragogy principles (Knowles 1980, 40–62).

Andragogy: Adults as Learners

In early childhood education, we often refer to pedagogy as the art and science of teaching children. Most educators view the pedagogical model as one in which teachers take a very active role in making decisions about what will be learned in the classroom and the activities that will be presented to children. Although early childhood educators feel strongly about each child's role in discovery and exploration, ultimately the teacher fills the role of expert resource and guide for the child's learning experience.

Andragogy evolved from the practices of educators who discovered that teaching adults was different from what they had

Spotlight on Adult Learning Theorists

As your interest in training grows, you may find it helpful to dig deeper into the work of some of these experts.

Cyril Houle
One of the pioneers of modern adult education, Houle is best known for his analysis of motivation in adult learning. Houle described adult learners as goal-oriented, activity-oriented, or learning-oriented. His most influential work is *The Inquiring Mind* (1961).

Allen Tough
A student of Houle, Tough is most closely associated with self-directed learning among adults and adult learning projects. Tough's work forms the major research basis for the current emphasis on self-direction in adult education.

David Kolb
Influenced by the ideas of Piaget, Dewey, Lewin, and others, Kolb focused on the role of experiential learning in adult education. His work resulted in a greater understanding of adult learning styles and preferences, along with the roles of reflection, experience, abstraction, and experimentation in adult learning experiences.

Paulo Freire
Freire's best-known work, *Pedagogy of the Oppressed* (1970), is considered a classic among adult educators. Freire is most closely associated with a philosophy of education called critical pedagogy and is well-known for his disdain of what he called the "banking theory" of education, in which students are little more than accounts to be filled with knowledge by their teachers.

Jack Mezirow
Mezirow, whose research and work complement that of Freire, established what is now known as transformation theory. Mezirow's work reinforces the belief that adults can be transformed using critical reflection, in which they find new ways of characterizing their experiences and assumptions. Mezirow's works include *Transformative Dimensions of Adult Learning* (1991) and *Fostering Critical Reflection in Adulthood* (1990).

Malcolm Knowles
Called the father of adult learning or the father of andragogy, Knowles popularized the concept of andragogy throughout North America in the 1960s and 1970s. Andragogy is loosely translated as *the art and science of helping adults learn* and is the theoretical model most often associated with contemporary adult education. Two of Knowles' works, *The Modern Practice of Adult Education: From Pedagogy to Andragogy* (1980) and *The Adult Learner* (with Elwood F. Holton III and Richard A. Swanson) (1973), are still used by many adult educators and trainers today.

known as teachers of children. As early as the 1930s, adult educators realized the life experiences and motivations of adults were different from those of children and that teaching methods should reflect those realizations. By the 1960s, European educators (and later, American educators) were using andragogy as a theoretical model for adult learning in contrast to the one used for child learning.

Andragogy and pedagogy are often compared on the basis of four areas: self-direction of the learner; experiences of the learner; motivation of the learner; and immediacy of the learning need. The chart that follows compares pedagogy and andragogy in these areas.

Assumptions about Pedagogy and Andragogy

	PEDAGOGY	ANDRAGOGY
Self-direction of the learner	Children are expected to be more dependent upon the teacher for direction in the learning process. Even children who are autonomous see the teacher as an expert guide in their learning experiences.	Adults generally are able to be more self-directed in their learning process. Adults are capable of setting and reaching learning goals, even when temporarily dependent upon other adults for direction or encouragement.
Experiences of the learner	Children bring fewer life experiences to the learning situation than their adult counterparts. Because of their youth, children simply have not experienced as wide a range of things from which they can draw on in learning.	Adults are expected to have accumulated a wide range of life experiences that they can apply to learning situations. Adults draw on these experiences when learning and are influenced by their meaning. Adults also appear to place high value on their life experiences and for this reason prioritize learning that includes experience over other kinds of learning.
Motivation of the learner	Children often appear to be motivated to learn a wide variety of information and for a wide variety of reasons. Children are equally interested in ideas and experiences that have little practical application and those that are highly useful. For example, children may love to learn highly technical names of dinosaurs despite the fact that they will never see or encounter a dinosaur in daily life.	Adults tend to favor learning experiences that are related to something they need to know or can readily use. Adult educators often focus time and energy on describing why the information meets the need-to-know test in order to motivate adult learning.

Assumptions about Pedagogy and Andragogy (*continued*)

	PEDAGOGY	ANDRAGOGY
Immediacy of the learning need	Children are interested in learning opportunities that may have no immediate connection to their daily lives. They find learning interesting for its own sake and often explore topics that will only be used in the distant future, if ever. For example, children study animals they do not own or see, historical events they have not experienced, and people they do not know as part of their subject matter education.	Adults favor learning that has an immediate application to their daily lives or situations. Adults favor application-based learning and learning activities that are action-oriented. Adults may even comment that they only learn if the information is hands-on and they can use it right away.

Andragogy or Pedagogy? Age Isn't Everything

As you read some of the principles of andragogy, you may be thinking they also describe good early childhood practice. If that is the case, don't be discouraged or confused. Like you, many educators of children have found they employ principles associated with andragogy more and more in their early childhood education teaching. While there can be no doubt that teaching young children is different from teaching adults, they are similar many ways. Good teachers know when to employ the tactics that best support their learners, and increasingly teachers think of pedagogy and andragogy as the two ends of a continuum. Many educators do not associate pedagogy with children and andragogy with adults at all; they see these two kinds of learning principles as useful when considering a learner of any age. Consider the model on page 33.

By considering the two extremes of this continuum, you can imagine that much of the learning for children and adults falls somewhere in the middle. For example, adults can undertake learning experiences that do not have immediate application. An adult might take a film history class or a computer class just for the fun of the learning experience. Similarly, children often learn things they need to know right away, such as the rules to a game or a particular word or phrase. Thus, it is easy to see that the distinctions between these two extremes can be less about the age of the learner and more about the learner's orientation toward the learning task.

A Continuum of Choices

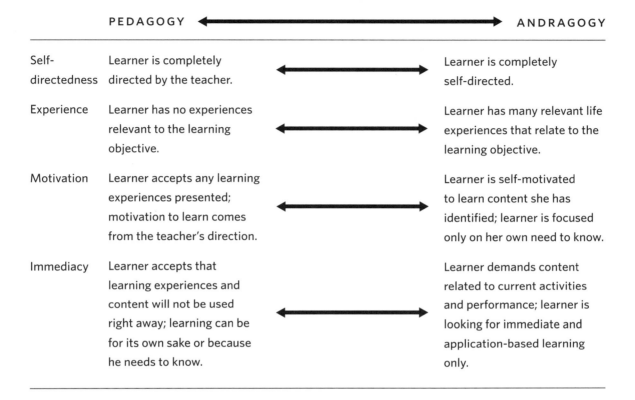

PEDAGOGY ⟵⟶ ANDRAGOGY

	PEDAGOGY		ANDRAGOGY
Self-directedness	Learner is completely directed by the teacher.		Learner is completely self-directed.
Experience	Learner has no experiences relevant to the learning objective.		Learner has many relevant life experiences that relate to the learning objective.
Motivation	Learner accepts any learning experiences presented; motivation to learn comes from the teacher's direction.		Learner is self-motivated to learn content she has identified; learner is focused only on her own need to know.
Immediacy	Learner accepts that learning experiences and content will not be used right away; learning can be for its own sake or because he needs to know.		Learner demands content related to current activities and performance; learner is looking for immediate and application-based learning only.

Summary

Organizing our thinking about the characteristics of adult learners helps us become more effective in planning for, designing, and implementing training activities. High-quality training is based on a thorough knowledge of adult learning principles, so trainers benefit from acquiring a rich understanding of the developmental characteristics of the learners they serve.

The three dimensions of knowledge described in NAEYC's position paper on developmentally appropriate practices offer a useful model for adult learning that will affect planning, design, implementation, and effectiveness of any training program. This model uses three building blocks for understanding adult learners:

- knowledge of age and stage characteristics
- knowledge of individual characteristics of adult learners
- knowledge of the social and cultural context that surrounds adult learning and the workplace

SECTION 2

Understanding Adult Learners

3

Knowledge of Age- and Stage-Related Human Characteristics in Adult Learning

Bob thought about his latest training innovation. "I paired Marie, our new teacher, with Frieda, who has been teaching here since we opened twelve years ago. The mentoring should have been a great opportunity for Marie to learn and Frieda to grow her leadership skills. But every time I observe them together, it sounds as if they come from different planets. They have nothing to talk about, no similar experiences to share. What happened?"

Using Andragogy in Your Training Practices

The principles of andragogy are important to your understanding of the characteristics of adult learners and your ability to effectively provide training for adults. The six core learning principles of andragogy and adult learning theory make up many of the best practices we associate with training.

Three Dimensions of Knowledge

```
              ┌─────────────────┐
              │  Knowledge of   │
              │  Age and Stage  │
              │ Characteristics │
    ┌─────────┴────────┬────────┴─────────┐
    │  Knowledge of    │   Knowledge of   │
    │   Individual     │  the Social and  │
    │ Characteristics  │     Cultural     │
    │                  │     Contexts     │
    └──────────────────┴──────────────────┘
```

Spotlight on Andragogy

Core Principles Related to Adult Learning

1. The Learner's Need to Know
2. The Learner's Self-Concept
3. The Learner's Experiences
4. The Learner's Readiness
5. The Learner's Orientation to the Learning Task
6. The Learner's Motivation

Becoming familiar with these principles and finding ways to embed them in your training design and presentation will help you to be a more effective educator of adults.

Although all adult learners are unique individuals, it is helpful to know that there are some consistent things about adult learners we can consider when we plan for them. As you read each of the descriptions of the core principles, think about the adults with whom you work each day. To what extent do they mirror these ideas? Where do you see differences in their motivations and needs?

The Learner's Need to Know

Adults prefer to understand why they need to know something as a motivation for learning. Have you ever heard trainees say, "Why does this matter?" Perhaps you remember echoes of "Will this be on the test?" from your college days. These are all expressions of adults wondering why they need to know.

As a trainer, you can motivate your trainees by explaining how they can use the knowledge and skills that are the focus of your training program. Many trainers include some description of the *need to know* in the introduction to a training session. Consider the last training session you conducted—what was the *need to know* for your trainees? How will your trainees benefit from participating in the training session? Would the information make their day in the classroom easier? Would children's experience in the classroom be enhanced? Would parents be more satisfied with the program?

Adults are motivated by training sessions that they believe will make their work easier, more successful, or more fulfilling.

One of your responsibilities as a trainer is to help trainees see the connection between the training you are providing and the benefits it will produce.

The Learner's Self-Concept

Adults see themselves as responsible for their own destinies and actions. They desire to be in charge of themselves and their learning. Adults may even actively resist training or education activities that they perceive to be forced on them. Trainees who ask if a meeting or training session is required may be expressing the level of resistance they feel to the activity. They may be trying to understand how much choice they have in selecting the learning activities that fit with their own image of their needs.

Allowing adults to take charge of their own learning motivates and encourages them to actively engage in the learning experience. Whenever practical, allow adults to make informed choices about participation in training. Even when training is mandatory, trainers can create an atmosphere of choice by providing a wide variety of options for trainees. For example, if your training session uses case studies as the basis of a role-play activity, provide a number of choices from which groups can choose rather than assigning a single case to each group. Simple gestures of respect such as this require very little extra preparation but go a long way in demonstrating to trainees that you respect their choices as adult learners.

The Learner's Experiences

Adults bring more experiences to learning activities, and their experiences have more variety than those found among children. Still, you may be wondering why experience matters if the topic you are teaching is new to your trainees or the skills you are teaching obviously aren't being used on a regular basis. Experiences matter because adults use them to ignite their learning. As adult learners, we naturally look for connections between our prior knowledge and experience and the new information.

As a trainer, you can use these connections to involve adults in learning and to commit them to exploring new ideas. For example, when one teacher has a good experience trying a new teaching technique, use her experience to begin a discussion about the technique to effectively engage others. When introducing a new idea, start with a related idea with which your trainees are already familiar. This familiarity validates learners' experiences and eases them into the new topic, idea, or process. For example, if the teachers you are training are already good at using songs and fingerplays during transitions or while children are waiting for the next activity to begin, use these experience to describe how they can use songs and fingerplays at stressful times or as bridges between activities. Using the trainees' own experiences draws them into the learning activity and engages their interest.

Failing to acknowledge the experiences of your learners can be disastrous. Much of adults' self-esteem is based on the experiences they have accumulated. Failing to acknowledge that your adult learners bring these experiences to their learning can be perceived as dismissive or even insulting. You will inevitably leave your learners feeling devalued and rejected if you treat them as though they are blank slates or sponges waiting to absorb the wisdom you have to share.

The Learner's Readiness

The old adage "timing is everything" holds true when working with adults. Adults learn best when they are well-prepared and ready for a new level and type of information. Think back to the first time you drove a car or operated a piece of equipment. In your first experience, you were probably only ready for some very basic instructions and a short experience using the gears and switches. At some point in your first training session, you realized you could not absorb any additional information, even though there was still much to learn; you were simply not ready to learn anything else at that moment. Being sensitive to the readiness of adult learners will help you to be a more effective trainer. Looking for cues that your trainees have absorbed all that they can in one session is important.

As a trainer, you must organize learning in ways that capitalize on trainees' readiness to learn. Consider for a moment those things teachers are most ready to learn. What might they ask for? What are they desperate to know? How can you use the needs of teachers to spark interest in learning and change? Later in this book, we will look at some of the ways you can assess the needs of the trainees you work with. Using them can help you to understand the level of readiness to learn among your trainees.

The Learner's Orientation to the Learning Task

Most adults look at learning as a means to an end. In general, adults approach learning activities as time spent solving problems, making their work easier, or improving their overall position in life. Adults tend to be goal-oriented toward learning: they seek out learning that helps them to meet a goal.

This orientation to learning can be very helpful to you as a trainer. Because most adults want to solve problems and make their lives easier, you can motivate them to participate in training by emphasizing the training outcomes that will match their goals. Consider the training session "Child Guidance Problem-Solving Session." Why might that session sound more appealing to adult learners than "Child Guidance Rules"? The promise of problem solving connects with many adults' innate desire to apply knowledge and accomplish a goal. Many of the hands-on, simulation activities we employ in adult learning are based on adults' orientation toward learning and their desire for application-oriented learning experiences.

Understanding the goals of your trainees will help you tap into their preferences. Later in the book, we will discuss individual professional development plans. Creating these plans for your trainees is a great way to document what you know about their needs and goals. Connecting each trainee's goals with the training experiences and activities you have planned creates a clear road map for learning success.

The Learner's Motivation

Just like children, adults are naturally motivated to learn. Adult motivations may be slightly different from those of children, but adults and children also share some of the same motivations. For example, adults are motivated to learn by recognition and the promise of satisfaction and a better quality of life. Training sessions that help adults find value in their work and make arduous tasks easier are often popular because they motivate and engage adult learners.

Uncovering the motivations of the adult learners you work with will help you connect to their needs. Consider the teachers in your typical training sessions. Which teachers are struggling with unfulfilled expectations? Who is interested in promotion? Which teachers are challenged by unsatisfying situations? Think of aspects of your training that could meet their needs. As you plan for individual training and group training experiences, consider these motivations; they will greatly increase the chances of engaging your learners.

When planning training sessions, trainers are careful to include opportunities for trainees to apply what they have learned in the session. These application activities often take the form of case studies or role-playing activities. In addition to providing practice, these activities enhance the motivation of adult learners because they demonstrate how the learning can be applied to benefit the trainees. As you construct training activities and experiences, look for ways to link your activities to the motivations of the trainees with whom you work. For example, if you have trainees who are interested in promotion to management positions, you can challenge their learning during training sessions by providing activities in which they must demonstrate leadership, decision making, or strategic thinking. This type of activity will motivate the trainee and provide you with additional insight into the abilities and learning needs of your trainees.

Putting Andragogy to Work

Let's consider the principles we have covered as they relate to a training topic. Assume you are considering a more widespread and vigorous use of family-style meal service in your program. You are preparing some training activities to promote the practice, to engage teachers in conversations about how the service could be used, and to discuss what obstacles they might

PRINCIPLE	IDEAS TO CONSIDER
The Learner's Need to Know	• Will teachers be expected to comply with this new practice? • Is there a rule, regulation, or policy that requires teachers to use family-style meal service? • How will using family-style meal service help teachers be more effective?
The Learner's Self-Concept	• Can teachers choose to opt in to the training and try family-style meal service? • Is learning the new way to serve meals and snacks a choice or is change required? • Can teachers set their own time lines for implementing what they have learned? • Can teachers choose when they are ready to use the new ideas?
The Learner's Experiences	• Have any teachers tried family-style meal service? • Can any teachers speak to its benefits? • Can any teachers describe how they overcame the challenges presented by family-style meal service? • Can teachers have time to try the ideas on a small scale before using them at every meal or in every class? • How open are teachers in general to changing the way they are doing things? Are changes in practice frequent or few?
The Learner's Readiness	• Have any teachers expressed interest in trying family-style meal service or other new ideas? • Do teachers have other basic classroom management skills that will make family-style meal service easy and practical? • Are the tools and supplies needed for family-style meal service available?
The Learner's Orientation to the Learning Task	• Have teachers expressed concerns or frustrations that could be solved by family-style meal service? • Are teachers interested in changing or improving practices? • Can you explain the benefits of family-style meal service in a way that meets teachers' needs?
The Learner's Motivation	• Are there accomplishments such as accreditation or promotion that interest teachers and might be tied to implementing the new meal service? • How will teachers be acknowledged for trying the new ideas? • How will attempts to try new ideas be recognized or rewarded? • What support can you provide to motivate teachers when they are learning the new skills needed for the family-style meal service?

encounter. The principles of andragogy might inform your practice as illustrated in the chart on page 42.

Now try using the principles of andragogy to think about a training topic you have been considering. Use the blank form on page 44 to capture some of your ideas about engaging your learners and appealing to their natural learning tendencies. Remember that all adult learners are not the same. Still, these principles give you a good starting point for thinking about the motivations and needs of your trainees. For a reproducible copy of Putting Andragogy to Work, see form 4 in the appendix.

Adult Ages and Stages

Up to this point, we have been talking about adults as a homogeneous group as though all adults are the same age, care about the same things, and have the same characteristics. Of course we know this is not the case. Some of the adults you train may be as young as eighteen years old and others may be well into their senior years. Their life experiences, expectations, interests, and habits are probably quite different. They have different levels of education, have traveled to different places, have held different jobs, and so on. Simply put, they are unique individuals. Nevertheless, sociologists and psychologists believe adults have similar tendencies at certain stages and within generations. These

tendencies can help you make some decisions about trainees.

As we grow, learn, and develop, we are influenced by our experiences. Think for a moment about some of the experiences that have changed the way you think about your job, program, and certain tasks or people you meet. Perhaps you once held a job in a very fast-paced environment and learned how to handle a wide variety of tasks that needed to be completed very quickly. This experience probably affects how you now handle unusually busy days. Perhaps you have had the opportunity to travel throughout the world. Your cultural experiences probably help guide the way you behave when you meet new people or are introduced to a family from another culture.

Think about the teachers you work with as a trainer. While you may not know the details of their life experiences, you may know a few of the influences that have helped shape their lives. These influences will affect the ways in which they work, the ways in which they approach caring for children, and the ways they see themselves as learners during training activities. For example, suppose that one of the teachers is someone who really struggled as a student. Perhaps she was unable to go to college or lacked the confidence to even apply to colleges following a difficult experience in high school. Certainly this negative experience would affect her confidence and might make her a more reluctant participant

Putting Andragogy to Work

· ·

Topic or training idea _____

PRINCIPLE	IDEAS TO CONSIDER
The Learner's Need to Know	• •
The Learner's Self-Concept	• •
The Learner's Experiences	• •
The Learner's Readiness	• •
The Learner's Orientation to the Learning Task	• •
The Learner's Motivation	• •

or a quieter, more self-conscious trainee. While we can never know all of the things that have influenced our trainees, we can assume that they have had rich lives filled with experiences that have shaped the way they behave, participate, and value training experiences. Their experiences make them unique individuals.

Luckily, as adults we have some unifying factors. Some aspects of our development are predictable. These common, predictable elements help trainers make some helpful assumptions about trainees that can substitute for knowing the personal details or life experiences of trainees. Unfortunately, trainings can't always be personalized or individualized.

The next two sections focus on two factors that help us make some assumptions about the needs of teachers. The first focuses on the influences that shape different generations of adults. The second focuses on the stages of development that influence teachers as they mature.

Generational Influences

Do you remember owning a television that did not have a remote control? What about a kitchen without a microwave? Today's college graduates have never lived without remotes, cell phones, microwaves, or desktop computers. The experiences and influences of this generation are quite different from those of people who grew up during the Cold War or those who have personal memories of the Vietnam War years, the Women's Movement, or the Watergate scandal. Perhaps you had a parent or a grandparent who lived through the Great Depression and never gave up the frugal practices of that era. The shared influences of each generation have an impact on how individuals view their work and their lives (Dittmann 2005, 54–55).

Baby Boomers

Baby boomers were born between 1946 and 1964. Research indicates that as employees, these people tend to value material rewards and see promotion as an important work goal. Baby boomer teachers value loyalty and expect to be rewarded for tenure and long service with one employer.

As trainees, baby boomers tend to value authority figures and subject matter experts. They are more familiar with the trainer-as-lecturer approach to instruction and may be reluctant to participate in training games, simulations, and other activities that they see as more closely linked with fun than learning. As trainees, baby boomers are the most likely to show reluctance to use technology for learning. Teachers in this generation may not be comfortable immediately embracing computer-based or online training.

Generation X

Generation X teachers were born between 1965 and 1981 (Lancaster and Stillman

2007). This generation is often described as skeptical and fiercely independent. Teachers from this generation place less value on loyalty and expect to change jobs, if not careers, several times during their professional lives. They place a high value on benefits, even over salary, and are highly motivated by work-life balance.

As trainees, people from generation X are naturally skeptical and tend to offer questions and even challenge the information presented to them. Because this generation places high value on flexibility, you should try to provide as much choice as possible in training times, location, and methods of training.

Millennials

The millennial generation, often referred to as generation Y, was born between 1982 and 2000. This generation has been heavily influenced by technology and expects it to be part of their work and family life. They are characterized as confident and optimistic and demonstrate a need for immediate gratification (Galagan 2006, 27–30).

As trainees, members of this generation place a high value on team activities, use technology eagerly, and expect to learn new things throughout their lives. They want consistent feedback and praise and enjoy fast-paced learning activities.

The Impact of Generational Influences

Consider for a moment the teachers you work with regularly or some of your recent trainees. Do the generational influences presented above seem consistent with your experience? Although individuals in all of these generational groups are unique, these broad generalizations may be helpful when you are preparing for the potential reactions they may have to your training content or methods. Suppose you are planning to use a highly interactive training game to introduce an important point during your training session. If you are expecting a large number of baby boomers in the session, how might they react? Logically, you can expect that some of these participants may view this activity with some skepticism. Using a strong introduction to entice and motivate these participants may help pave the way for their successful participation.

One of the most important considerations to keep in mind is to focus on the strengths of each generation. It is easy to become frustrated by the work habits or tendencies of any single generation, especially if you are not a member of it. But as a trainer, you must focus on the strengths of that generation and the individuals with whom you are working. Keep in mind the natural loyalty of baby boomer trainees, the creativity and technological savvy of gen Xers, and the confidence and flexibility of millennials. Tap into these positive attributes by matching training techniques to your trainees' generational tendencies.

Stages of Teacher Development
....

Somara reviewed the training session she had prepared for the staff meeting tomorrow night. "Guidance basics again," she thought. "Well, Millie and John have heard this six times. I wonder if I should let the veteran teachers leave early? They must get tired of hearing the same introductory sessions over and over every fall." At that moment, Millie entered the room. "Why don't you let me teach the session? I've got it down by now," Millie said.

In addition to the stages of adult development that influence employees in early childhood programs, trainees are also affected by their teaching experience. Common sense tells us that a teacher who is new to the profession probably has different needs for training and professional development than a teacher who has worked in the profession for many years. In fact, a great deal of research supports the notion that teachers progress through predictable stages as they mature. Lilian Katz first proposed four stages of teacher development to describe teachers in the early childhood profession: survival, consolidation, renewal, and maturity (Katz 1995, 203–210).

Stage 1: Survival

Teachers in the earliest stage of development are looking for ways to apply all they have learned about working with young children. These teachers may be somewhat overwhelmed by the complexity of managing a classroom, planning program elements, and working with children with unique needs and interests. Although stage 1 teachers have great enthusiasm, they can feel unprepared and overwhelmed by the realities of working in the profession.

Training for stage 1 teachers revolves around day-to-day dilemmas and tactics and methods to help them apply what they have learned. Teachers in this survival stage also seek training as a means of support and to affirm their abilities and motivation to teach. Trainers can provide a valuable service to these beginning teachers by providing encouragement as well as technical assistance and skill training. Mentoring and one-on-one coaching are particularly good training techniques for teachers early in their development.

Stage 2: Consolidation

By about the second year of teaching, most teachers have mastered the basic skills needed to survive day-to-day in the classroom. These teachers are ready to focus their training time on more complex and challenging questions. Stage 2 teachers often focus on children who do not fit their expectations for on-level development or those who present special challenges to classroom management.

Because teachers at this stage have some classroom experiences and successes, your training efforts should acknowledge what they already know and can do. Look for opportunities to value these teachers by asking them to share with newer teachers what they have learned or what they have accomplished. Expect that teachers at this stage will be looking for strategies that address children with challenging behaviors or developmental delays. While mentoring and coaching continue to be good training techniques for stage 2 teachers, you can also offer them guided and self-paced study and participation in conference sessions or other instructor-led experiences.

Stage 3: Renewal

After several years in the classroom, teachers may become a bit restless. At the very least, they are ready to add some new ideas to their teaching methods. Stage 3 teachers are comfortable with their ability to handle the everyday tasks associated with teaching and the unique needs of the children they serve. At the same time, teachers in this stage are still looking for new ideas and opportunities to try new things. These teachers know they still have a great deal to learn about teaching and the early childhood profession. Their self-confidence supports interest in new and perhaps more advanced ways of doing things.

Teachers at this renewal stage of development can be very exciting for you to work with. These teachers have enough foundational knowledge to explore new ideas and are often open to examining their own practice. They can benefit greatly from reading materials, conferences and seminars, professional groups, and communities of practice. They also appreciate training sessions in which they can explore new ideas and use what they know to support others.

Stage 4: Maturity

It is impossible to predict how many years are required for a teacher to reach maturity. However, the third to fifth years of teaching is often thought as the period in which teachers mature in their practice. Mature teachers are comfortable, confident, and even philosophical about their teaching practice. They not only can handle daily challenges, but they have also mastered many of the complex issues present in the early childhood classroom. These mature teachers are often mentors for other teachers and may even be ready to seek promotion to other positions such as program director or curriculum specialist.

Although these teachers have reached maturity, they can still benefit from training and professional development experiences. The training needs of mature teachers are often focused on preparation for their next professional level. Mature teachers may be interested in opportunities to focus on program development or management tasks.

Stage 1	Stage 2	Stage 3	Stage 4
Survival	Consolidation	Renewal	Maturity

Many mature teachers seek out opportunities to train others as a means to enhance their own development. Another opportunity for mature teachers can be found in leadership experiences such as leading a team to plan a center event or to implement a new program or practice.

The stages of teacher development should be thought of as points on a continuum. Teachers do not leave one stage and enter the next stage as though each were a separate room in a house. Teachers progress through the stages slowly and may simultaneously exhibit characteristics from more than one stage of development. Consider the continuum below. Think about each of the teachers in your program. Where would each one fall on this continuum?

Teachers may also move among the stages of development in response to changes in their teaching milieu. For example, a teacher who has reached the level of renewal or maturity may need to focus on survival or consolidation tasks if her program makes a significant change in curriculum or philosophy. It is important, then, to think of the stages of teacher development as interrelated and evolving.

Who Are the Teachers You Train?

You have thought about each of the teachers you train as a unique individual with her own needs, interests, characteristics, and talents. You have considered the generational influences and stages of development that shape each person. Now you should create an individual profile for each of the teachers you train. Use the form that follows to capture what you know about each of them. This information is another important piece of your training plan. For a reproducible copy of Training Plan: Individual Teacher Profile, see form 5 in the appendix.

Special Considerations for Orienting New Teachers

Angéle couldn't wait for Susan to arrive. She loved the first day a new teacher worked in the program. It was fun to tour the classrooms, introduce all the teachers, and see the friendships begin. Angéle took out her notes from Susan's interview. She reminded herself, "I've got to take extra time when I cover the procedures for addressing food allergies. Susan has two children in her class with severe allergies."

Training Plan: Individual Teacher Profile

· ·

Date _____

Teacher's name _____

Years of experience _____

Educational background _____

Generational influences _____

Stage of teacher development _____

Unique talents, interests, experiences, and characteristics _____

_____

_____

_____

Unique challenges and needs _____

_____

_____

_____

Notes _____

_____

_____

_____

_____

_____

_____

_____

_____

When a new teacher joins a program, a great deal of time and many resources have already been invested in recruiting and selecting her. The first impressions a teacher receives during her initial days and weeks should be positive and set the stage for a long and successful engagement with the program. Orientation makes a lasting impression on a newly hired teacher, so it deserves thoughtful planning and careful implementation.

Teachers who are new to a program have some special needs that are worthy of consideration. Some who are new to a program are clearly stage 1 teachers in the early years of their teaching careers. Other new teachers bring a wealth of experience to their new assignment. The following considerations will help you plan training for teachers who are adjusting to a new program and work environment.

Start with the Information Learned during the Selection Process

Résumés, interviews, and job previews are great opportunities to investigate the initial training needs of newly hired teachers. Besides using these to determine if the teacher is the best fit for the position, you can use these opportunities to understand what training needs she may have. What answers did this teacher give that hinted at developmental needs? What experiences are missing from her résumé that she will need to acquire?

Plan for All of the Compliance Requirements of the Program

Evaluate your new employee orientation plan to be sure it meets all of the requirements for the licensing agency, accreditation, and agencies or auspices that influence the program. Remember that the National Association for the Education of Young Children accreditation has specific areas that must be included in your training plan for new employees (NAEYC 2005, 52–53).

Create a Layered Plan to Avoid Overload

Even the most enthusiastic new employee can only master a limited amount of information at one time. Develop an orientation plan that extends over weeks (or even months) so you can introduce information as it is needed and mastered by new teachers. Although such an extended orientation takes longer, the impact and effectiveness of your training will improve.

Don't Assume

When new employees arrive with experience and educational credentials, it is tempting to assume that they are ready to begin in the classroom. Remember that early childhood programs differ in curriculum, quality, and rules that affect polices and procedures. Take time to orient each new teacher to be sure that she has the best chance of success within your program.

Socialization Matters

One of the most critical needs of teachers new to a program is socialization. To reach their full potential, all teachers need to feel a sense of belonging and camaraderie in a program, no matter their stage as teachers. Besides planning for training of knowledge and skills, put some thought into how new teachers are welcomed to the program. Consider assigning a buddy to a newly hired teacher for the first few days or weeks. During orientation, be sure to cover the little things that signal to a newly hired teacher that she is part of the team. For example, introduce her to all of her new colleagues, point out a place where she can store her belongings, and discuss the dress code and the typical dress of other teachers in the program.

Make a Positive First Impression

Remember the adage "You never get a second chance to make a good first impression"? It applies equally to the newly hired teacher and to the program. Her first impression extends beyond the interview to the first few days of work. Plan carefully to ensure a positive first experience by creating a thorough, written plan. Meet the newly hired teacher when she arrives for her first day of work, and take some time to describe the orientation plan before beginning training activities. Enlist the teacher's input about other training items she wants included in order to feel comfortable and ready for work. These relatively simple gestures will have a positive and lasting impression on any newly hired teacher.

The worksheet that follows is based on the NAEYC's accreditation criteria for initial orientation (NAEYC 2005, 6.A.03). These describe specific categories of information that must be introduced to each new employee in the program. These provide a good overview of orientation needs for any program. Use this worksheet to describe the ways in which each of these aspects will be introduced to new employees. For a reproducible copy of Orientation Worksheet, see form 6 in the appendix.

Summary

Adults share certain characteristics as learners. Understanding these characteristics can help you prepare training experiences that are more effective and that achieve your objectives. For example, planning for the adult learner's need for immediacy and practical application of training experiences is likely to enhance trainees' engagement and overall satisfaction.

Trainers benefit from understanding the characteristics of different age groups and the developmental stages of teachers. Knowledge of these influences provides valuable background information for trainers when they are diagnosing the needs of trainees and anticipating how trainees are likely to respond to different training methods and topics.

Orientation Worksheet

For each aspect of the orientation, describe the materials that will be used and the way in which the information will be introduced.

Program philosophy, values, and goals	Materials _____ _____ Methods of introduction _____ _____
Expectations for ethical conduct	Materials _____ _____ Methods of introduction _____ _____
Health, safety, and emergency procedures	Materials _____ _____ Methods of introduction _____ _____
Individual needs of children in the classroom assignment	Materials _____ _____ Methods of introduction _____ _____
Accepted guidance and classroom management techniques	Materials _____ _____ Methods of introduction _____ _____
Daily activities and routines of the program	Materials _____ _____ Methods of introduction _____ _____

Program curriculum	Materials _____
	Methods of introduction _____
Child abuse and neglect reporting procedures	Materials _____
	Methods of introduction _____
Program polices and procedures	Materials _____
	Methods of introduction _____
NAEYC Early Childhood Program Standards	Materials _____
	Methods of introduction _____
Regulatory requirements	Materials _____
	Methods of introduction _____
Follow-up training to expand on initial orientation	Materials _____
	Methods of introduction _____

Adapted from *NAEYC Early Childhood Standards and Accreditation Criteria: The Mark of Quality in Early Childhood Education,* Standard 6, Criterion 6.A.03. Copyright © 2005 by the National Association for the Education of Young Children.

CHAPTER 4

Knowledge of Individual Strengths, Interests, and Needs

Michelle looked at the list of teachers for Saturday's training session. Everyone was really excited about the session she had planned on emergent curriculum. But, she knew that Sue could really use some time on guidance techniques, and Francis had requested more information on time management and planning practices. "I guess Saturday's session is just the beginning," she thought.

In previous chapters, we briefly mentioned the roles of regulatory compliance and program goals in planning trainings. The third priority to consider when crafting a training plan is the training needs of individual teachers. Each of these three priorities must have a place within the overall training plan for the program. Besides your knowledge of adult learners,

Three Dimensions of Knowledge

	Knowledge of Age and Stage Characteristics
Knowledge of Individual Characteristics	Knowledge of the Social and Cultural Contexts

you must understand how to assess training needs, select training methods, and plan for professional development to meet the needs of teachers. The sections that follow address these important topics.

Assessing Individual Needs

Obviously, the first step in developing training for teachers is to assess their individual training needs. Assessment will help you hone in on the areas of practice that can be improved through training and assist you in developing a plan that matches each teacher's unique needs. There are many sources of information you can use to assess teachers' training needs.

The Selection Process

A great deal of information is gathered about the potential new hire during selection and hiring. Use this information to identify the areas in which the teacher can use support and training. For example, if the newly hired teacher has never worked in a full-day program and will do so now, she may need training on routines such as meals and naptime.

Performance Appraisals

Most programs conduct performance appraisals on a regular basis. These reviews of an employee's work often help determine salary adjustments, promotions, and new assignments. Performance appraisals also can be helpful in identifying training needs because they usually include conversations about the teacher's development goals. Use these conversations to identify and plan for training that can help the teacher achieve those goals.

Classroom Observations

Regular observations of teachers in action present some of the best opportunities to identify training needs. During these observations, be sure to identify the teacher's strengths and weaknesses that could be corrected by training.

A wide variety of tools can be used to conduct classroom observations. You might choose to use a standardized tool, such as the Early Childhood Environment Rating Scale (ECERS), or you might construct an observation tool of your own. Use different tools for different situations. For example, you might use a very short checklist to observe one aspect of the program and a longer, more comprehensive tool for another. Specific classroom observations can help identify how much training is needed and the specific skills or knowledge that must be addressed in order for the training to change the teacher's performance. The form that follows is an example of a short assessment that can be used to gauge a teacher's leadership during group time. For a reproducible copy of Observation: Group Time, see form 7 in the appendix.

Observation: Group Time

Check the box that best describes the extent to which each behavior is observed.
1 = to a very little extent, **2** = to a little extent, **3** = to a great extent, **4** = to a very great extent

	1	2	3	4
Children are invited to the group time in an organized and thoughtful way.				
The group-time routine is familiar to the children; the children know what to expect.				
The group-time activities are appropriate to the children's level of development and interests.				
The group-time activities are presented in a way that is engaging to the children.				
The teacher's planning meets the needs of the children.				
The group time ends in a logical manner; it is clear to the children how to transition to the next activity.				

Comments _____

_____

_____

_____

_____

Observation tools covering a variety of teaching tasks and classroom practices can help identify broader areas in which training might be needed.

Surveys

Surveys can be excellent tools for gathering information from teachers about their training needs. They not only help you collect information about teachers' own perceptions of their needs but demonstrate to teachers that their opinions and ideas are important parts of the planning process.

Surveys can take a variety of forms; they do not have to be complex to be effective. The examples that follow demonstrate three types of surveys. The first asks a few open-ended questions. Teachers' answers to these questions provide you with direction about their training needs. Open-ended surveys are helpful when you have little sense of direction about teachers' potential needs. The drawback of this type of survey is that the amount and type of data collected can be hard to work with and some teachers may see a survey of this kind as time-consuming to respond to. This perception may diminish their response rate and the quality of their responses.

The open-ended survey that follows can be used to solicit general information about teachers' training needs. For a reproducible copy of Training Survey, see form 8 in the appendix.

A second way to survey teachers' training needs is to identify some potential areas of training and to ask teachers to respond to these areas. To create a survey of this kind, you will need to know some of the areas of training that might interest the teachers you serve or the areas in which they have demonstrated training needs.

Surveys that focus on one or a few areas of training typically use either rating or ranking scales. Rating scales ask teachers to rate their perceptions of training needs in each area. When responding to a rating survey, teachers can express a high degree of interest in many or all of the training topics. This type of survey does not ask teachers to compare the areas of training or to identify the relative importance of areas. An example of a survey using rating scales is shown on page 60. For a reproducible copy of Training Survey: Sample Using Rating, see form 9 in the appendix.

Surveys using rankings ask teachers to assess their training needs relative to each other. When using a ranking survey, teachers must prioritize their training needs. To create a ranking survey, you must have some initial ideas about the areas of training that are appropriate to the teachers you intend to survey and eventually train. An example of a survey using rankings is shown on page 61. For a reproducible copy of Training Survey: Sample Using Ranking, see form 10 in the appendix.

Using Data

A third source of information about the training needs of teachers may be data that are generated by the program. Some

Training Survey

Teacher's name _____

I feel my strengths as a teacher include _____

_____

_____

_____

_____

Some of the areas I feel I can improve include _____

_____

_____

_____

_____

I would like additional information or training on the following topics _____

_____

_____

_____

_____

_____

_____

Training Survey: Sample Using Rating

Dear Teacher:

   We are currently planning our training offerings for the upcoming year. In order to create plans that meet your individual needs, we are asking for your help in gathering information about your interests.

Rate your level of interest in receiving training on the topics listed below.

Teacher's name _____

S = Strongly Agree   **A** = Agree   **N** = Neutral   **D** = Disagree   **SD** = Strongly Disagree

I am interesting in training about:	S	A	N	D	SD
Child guidance techniques					
Classroom planning					
Literacy activities					
Math activities					
Classroom routines, such as meals					
Early childhood theory					
Other: _____					

Training Survey: Sample Using Ranking

Dear Teacher:

We are currently planning our training offerings for the upcoming year. In order to create plans that meet your individual needs, we are asking for your help in gathering information about your interests.

Rank your level of interest in receiving training on the topics listed below. Rank each item from 1 to 5, with 1 representing your highest priority and 5 your lowest priority. Use each number only once.

Teacher's name _____

Training topics	Rank
Classroom planning	
Conducting child assessment	
Planning for family conferences	
Planning for outdoor play	
Confronting challenging child behaviors	

of the kinds of data that may be helpful in understanding your teachers' training needs include child assessments, parent surveys, enrollment rates, accreditation reports, or ratings from the use of state's standard quality rating systems. These data may help verify some observations that have already been made about teachers' strengths and challenges, or they may uncover some unidentified areas. For example, parent surveys may indicate that parents do not feel they are communicating well with one of the teachers in the program. Although communication may not have been identified by the teacher or the program director as an area of concern, the parents' perceptions are valid reasons to view this as a potential training need.

Meeting Individual Needs through Training

Renata reflected on her observations in the toddler room yesterday. She was surprised to see so many violations of the program's rules for hand washing and food service. "I guess we'll need to cover hand washing at the staff meeting," she said to her colleague Marsha. Marsha replied, "It's too bad; everyone else really gets it. I hate to keep training on that topic."

One of the most common errors trainers and program directors make is to address individual training needs in group trainings. Using group training primarily for the benefit of a few teachers is rarely a good idea. The teachers who need the training often miss the point, and the teachers who don't need the training often resent the training (and the trainer) because they feel their valuable time has been wasted on unnecessary topics.

Individual training needs can be effectively met through a variety of training methods. Each of the training methods that follow can be used to strengthen individual knowledge, skills, and attitudes and to enhance an individual teacher's performance.

Self-Study

When training needs are unique to one individual, self-study can be an excellent training method. Self-study can include the use of reading materials, online training classes, computer-based training, videos/DVDs, conference sessions, project work, or for-credit classes. When planning a course of self-study for a teacher, keep in mind the following:

1. Develop a written self-study plan with the teacher. Self-study will only be successful when the teacher agrees to the plan and its details. Outline the goals of the self-study, what is to be done, and when it must be completed. Include as much detail as possible. Both you and the teacher should sign the plan.
2. Check regulatory requirements for self-study options. Some state licensing

agencies allow self-study to be counted toward annual in-service training requirements; others do not. Be sure to check your state's requirements before developing a plan with a teacher. If you choose to use self-study, even if it may not count toward in-service requirements, clearly explain the situation to the teacher.

3. Provide as many of the necessary materials as possible. The ability of a teacher to successfully complete a self-study training assignment is greatly enhanced when the task is relatively uncomplicated and offers few obstacles. Providing reading materials, computer access, and other resources increases the chances that a teacher will be able to successfully complete a self-study assignment.

4. Check in regularly with the teacher. As with any other assignment, regular feedback and follow-up increase the likelihood of successful completion of a self-study assignment.

5. Discuss the results. At the assignment's completion, take time to discuss the results with the teacher. What did she learn? How will she change her practices? Did she encounter any surprises? What new information did she uncover? Would others in the program benefit from this training?

Mentoring or Coaching

Mentoring or coaching is generally thought of as on-the-job training. It can be very effective in enhancing the performance of an individual teacher or a group of teachers who work together. Many quality-enhancement projects use mentoring or coaching to provide technical assistance to programs.

Mentoring or coaching can be conducted by a trainer, a supervisor, or an experienced peer such as a master teacher. A best practice associated with mentoring is agreeing at the beginning of the mentoring on the goals of the relationship and how communication will be organized. Protégées and mentors should agree on how often they will meet, when observations will be conducted, and how long the mentoring is expected to continue. Shared expectations create trust and help mentors and protégées avoid misunderstanding and disappointment.

Job Aids

One of the simplest and most overlooked ways to improve the performance of one or a few teachers is with job aids. Examples of job aids are hand-washing directions posted at a hand-washing sink, a recipe for mixing cleaning solution attached to the containers in which the ingredients are stored, and a chart that shows how to organize children's cots during naptime to meet the licensing regulations governing the program. Job aids support performance by providing information in the work environment where and when it is most needed.

Because teaching in an early childhood program is complex and requires knowledge and skills in a wide variety of areas, job aids can be very helpful in addressing information that is not easily remembered or is not used often enough to be committed to memory. Job aids are also helpful in situations in which there is little or no room for error. In these cases, job aids can provide the details that are critical to success. Additional information on constructing job aids can be found on page 115.

Small-Group Training

When training needs are shared among several teachers, small-group learning activities are a good choice. Small-group activities can include traditional, instructor-led training with a few participants or other activities that more closely resemble self-study. For example, a small group of teachers could address a training need by becoming involved in a group in which a book related to the training need is read and discussed among the trainees.

Individual Professional Development Plans

. . . .

Ari studied the brochure for the local early childhood conference. She looked up and asked Jaden, "What was it you said I should look for at the next conference? Was it something related to literacy?" Jaden thought for a moment and replied, "That sounds right. Let's check your plan in your file to be sure. You want to get the most out of this conference."

Although most teachers consider themselves lifelong learners and intend to continue to grow and develop throughout their careers, few have well-developed, written individual professional development plans. These plans not only formalize a teacher's good intentions but also help the trainer or program director plan and provide feedback in support of the teacher's needs.

The individual professional development plan combines the teacher's interests and perceptions of her training needs with the priorities established by her supervisor. The plan brings together what has been learned during the assessment of the teacher's needs and the priorities of the program. Creating the individual professional development plan involves the following steps:

1. Assess the teacher's training needs.
2. Solicit the teacher's perceptions of his training needs through conversation or survey.
3. Discuss the potential areas of training, and establish three or four training goals. Enhance goal setting by using the SMART goal formula discussed on page 12.
4. Identify any common training goals among teachers in the same program. Teachers who share training goals may be able to collaborate during training.
5. Research one or two training methods that address each training goal.

6. Meet together with the teacher to craft the individual professional development plan. Agree on the methods and time line for accomplishing each training goal.

7. Provide the resources needed to accomplish training tasks.

8. Check in regularly while the training is underway.

9. Recognize and celebrate accomplishments when they occur.

10. Set new goals as existing goals are accomplished.

The following form illustrates how an individual professional development plan can be organized. Professional development plans for the teachers in a program are part of the overall training plan. For a reproducible copy of Individual Professional Development Plan, see form 11 in the appendix.

Summary

Understanding the natural tendencies of adult learners and the stages of development that influence teachers as they learn and grow is the first step in addressing trainees' needs. The second step is assessing and planning for the unique needs and interests of individual teachers.

Individual needs can be assessed in a number of ways. Trainers use interviews, surveys, observations, and program data to construct a complete picture of trainees' individual needs. Trainers include the perceptions of trainees while developing training goals and plans so that the individual for whom it is designed is committed to the plan. Working together, the trainee and the trainer make use of a wide variety of training methods to enhance professional development and the quality of the program.

Individual Professional Development Plan

Teacher's name _____

Compliance training required _____

_____

Results of training needs assessment—areas of interest,
needs, and current challenges to be addressed by training _____

_____

_____

Development Goal #1 _____

_____

Training methods and activities   Deadline

1. _____   _____

2. _____   _____

3. _____   _____

4. _____   _____

Development Goal #2 _____

_____

Training methods and activities   Deadline

1. _____   _____

2. _____   _____

3. _____   _____

4. _____   _____

Development Goal #3 _____

_____

Training methods and activities   Deadline

1. _____   _____

2. _____   _____

3. _____   _____

4. _____   _____

Development Goal #4 _____

_____

Training methods and activities   Deadline

1. _____   _____

2. _____   _____

3. _____   _____

4. _____   _____

5 Knowledge of Social and Cultural Contexts in Training

Jessica considered the events of the evening. She was glad to have completed another training session and felt confident that many of the teachers learned about the new curriculum they would begin using next month. Still, she felt uneasy about calling the evening a success. "Maria and Beth never seem to participate. Even when I ask for their ideas, they offer a word or *two at most. I wish they were more connected to the rest of the team."*

Early childhood programs are supported by a group of individuals who work closely together to meet the needs of children and families. These individuals come to know

Three Dimensions of Knowledge

Knowledge of
Age and Stage
Characteristics

Knowledge of
Individual
Characteristics

Knowledge of
the Social and Cultural
Contexts

and rely on each other every day. Friendships often develop among the teachers in a program, and conflicts are inevitable. Social relationships affect the way a program functions and the culture that develops in it. The culture of a program can be described as the characteristics that define its environment, norms, atmosphere, behaviors, and interactions.

The social and cultural contexts of the program shape the content of your trainings and the way content is presented. First, part of the program's culture is defined by its commitment to continuous improvement and professional development. In programs in which a high value is placed on these commitments, more trainings are expected and offered. Teachers in such programs seek out training opportunities and enthusiastically participate in them. Programs in which training and professional development are valued are also more likely to recognize and reward training or teachers' educational accomplishments.

Second, the atmosphere within a program may influence the way in which training is organized and offered. For example, some programs have developed a culture in which everyone expects that training needs will be provided for teachers. In other programs, the culture is such that teachers are expected to use their own resources to meet their training needs.

A third way in which the program's culture and social environments affect training is in the way that training is conducted. In

some programs, the goals of training are development of skills and knowledge and support of a positive work culture. In these programs, training sessions often include icebreakers, team activities, and social events such as celebrations of birthdays, anniversaries, or other occasions. These programs use training to build knowledge, skills, social networks, and collegial connections.

Training environments are influenced by the beliefs, values, and attitudes that employees bring to the training. These social and cultural contexts determine how the employees respond to the training topics or methods. Trainers should be aware of the following considerations to fully understand the impact of these contexts on training.

Program Structure and Mission

One of the important influences on a program's social and cultural contexts is the structure and mission of the program. For example, the Head Start program has a different purpose and mission than a faith-based program. The program's mission influences the way in which priorities are set and determines the behaviors that will be valued.

The culture of a program is established by its mission and has an important influence on the trainer and the role of training. For example, a Head Start training is likely to include a session devoted to Head

Start regulations, policies, and procedures. Similarly, an early childhood program that includes parent education in its mission is likely to devote at least part of its training plan to the skills and knowledge required to involve and educate parents.

The mission and structure of any early childhood program may subtly influence training in other ways. You may find that some programs value innovation—and as a result, they embrace frequent change. In these programs, training sessions often include cutting-edge topics and use highly creative training techniques. Other programs may value standardization. Training in these programs is likely to be formal and to adhere to specific training outlines or materials so that all teachers receive and maintain the same content and approach.

If you are new to a program or work with a variety of programs, it is important to understand how training fits into the culture of each program. Ask yourself the following questions to understand how training fits into the program's culture:

- What is the mission of the program? Is training or professional development mentioned in the mission statement?
- Does the program pride itself on being innovative, current, or state-of-the-art?
- Are teachers in the program active in professional organizations?
- How have teachers from the program fulfilled their training and professional development obligations in the past?

- Is there any regularly scheduled time for teacher meetings, training sessions, or professional gatherings?
- Does the program maintain professional resources for teachers, such as journals or resource books?
- Does the program's budget demonstrate a commitment to teacher training or professional development?
- Does the program offer regularly scheduled paid time for professional development?
- Has the program offered a training plan in the past? Does it provide individual professional development plans for teachers?

There are no right or wrong answers to these questions; use them to gather information on how training has been used and valued in the program's culture.

Training as a Means to Support Social Interaction

Ramona eased into the back of the meeting room. "What luck," she thought, "a teachers' meeting on my first day of work. I wish I could remember some names. Everyone else seems to know each other."

Using training to influence the social and cultural contexts of a program should strengthen the relationships among teachers. Perhaps you can recall training you attended in which one of the goals was for the trainees to get to know each other better. Perhaps you have participated in training designed to improve cultural awareness and understanding. The use of ice-breakers and team-building activities during training sessions is considered best practice for building a positive social climate. These are examples of training activities that work to influence the social and cultural contexts of the program.

Ice-Breakers

Trainers have historically used short, warm-up activities at the beginning of training sessions. These activities are helpful to trainers because they

- invite participation.
- lighten the mood of the group.
- signal to the group that the session will require involvement.
- break down barriers between participants.
- increase familiarity among participants, thereby decreasing self-consciousness.

There are hundreds of resources that describing ice-breakers for training sessions. Many trainers also use tried-and-true party games, such as finding matching pairs or scavenger hunts, as training session ice-breakers. While ice-breakers are common, they are not required. The following

principles will help guide your use of ice-breakers.

Use Ice-Breakers Only with a Goal in Mind

Never use ice-breakers simply to get things started or to fill up valuable training time. Plan an ice-breaker for the session if you have such goals as these:

- Learning participant's names. Many ice-breakers are helpful for making introductions or practicing names of trainees.
- Inviting involvement and participation. Using an ice-breaker to engage the trainees is particularly important if the group is known to be reluctant about participating. If the group eagerly participates in active learning, an ice-breaker may not be needed.
- Introducing or previewing the topic. Using an ice-breaker that cleverly introduces the topic can be a fun and creative way to kick off a training session. For example, you might play a scavenger hunt in which trainees locate various supplies used for hand washing as a way to introduce a session on that topic.
- Understanding what trainees already know. Ice-breakers can be used to assess trainees' existing knowledge. Puzzles, word games, and other game show-style games can be enjoyable warm-up activities that also give the trainer some insight into the trainees' knowledge and skills.

Start Off Safely

Never start a session with an activity that could embarrass, frighten, or humiliate trainees. The ice-breaker must set a positive first impression by being safe, achievable, and relatively risk-free.

Keep Ice-Breakers Appropriate to the Length of the Training Session

One of the biggest drawbacks of ice-breakers is the amount of time they can consume. When training time is scarce, be cautious about using one. Even very simple ice-breakers can take up more of your valuable training time than you intend. When conducting a very short training session, it may be best to forego the ice-breaker entirely.

Simple Is Better

Avoid using overly complex games or activities as ice-breakers. Adults take some time to shift into learning mode. Starting a session with complex rules, multiple steps, or confusing terminology can be counterproductive.

Practice Makes Perfect

Always practice an ice-breaker before you use it in a training session. Try the activity out on family or friends to be sure you can give the directions comfortably and clearly. Have the correct props on hand and anticipate any potential stumbling blocks, such as an uneven number of participants or reluctant trainees. Remember, ice-breakers begin your training session, and you are likely to be a bit nervous when you start. Practice so that you feel confident and can start your session smoothly.

Team-Building Activities

Besides ice-breakers, team-building exercises are often used during training sessions to address social goals. These activities are typically designed to

- promote teamwork.
- increase familiarity among team members.
- develop cooperation skills.
- enhance communication.
- build conflict-resolution skills.

As with ice-breakers, resources describing team-building activities abound. The following principles can help you to select and use them to your advantage:

Plan Team-Building Activities with a Goal in Mind

All team-builders share the basic goal of increasing teamwork and cooperation among participants. In addition to this basic goal, team-building activities can be selected to support a variety of behaviors including problem solving, leadership, creativity, and risk taking. Choose activities that introduce or reinforce behaviors that match your training goals for the group.

Infuse Content into Team-Building Activities

Because training time is usually precious, team-building activities should use content appropriate to the session. For example, a training session addressing process art for children may use a team-building activity in which teachers build a sculpture together.

Use Competition Wisely

Some groups thrive on a little healthy competition while others find competitive activities uncomfortable. If you are unfamiliar with the group for whom you are providing training, check with one of the group's leaders about ways competition has been used in the past. When you do choose to use a competitive activity, be clear about the rules of the activity and how winners will be decided.

Decide in Advance How You Will Determine Teams

Teams can be configured in a number of ways. Consider each of the following:

- Random teams. Ask the group to count off. For example, if you need four groups, ask the participants to each call out the numbers one to four in sequence. Continue until each participant has been assigned a number. Group those with the same number into teams. There are also many creative ways to create randomly assigned teams; these can be found in resources on team building.

- Representative teams. Sometimes it is helpful to create teams that represent all of the roles in the larger group. Creating teams that include one infant program teacher, one toddler program teacher, one preschool teacher, and one school-age teacher is an example of an often-used representative team for an early childhood training session. Decide the composition of the teams in advance and assign participants on the basis of their roles.

- Self-selected teams. When the composition of the teams is unimportant, you can allow the participants to create teams on their own. Give clear directions about how many participants may be on each team.

Think Carefully about Physical Activity in Team Building and Games

Team-building activities or games that involve strenuous physical activity present two challenges. First, some participants may be unwilling to become involved in such activities. Expect resistance, and plan alternate activities for unwilling trainees. Second, the uneven ability levels among participants can present challenges. Some trainees may be unable to participate fully or may even risk injury by becoming involved.

Ice-breakers and team-builders are used by trainers to promote social interactions during training. Trainers also use other techniques such as group work, activities, or discussions that involve social interactions. Additional information on these presentation techniques is provided in chapter 7.

Social and Cultural Influences in Training Sessions

The content of training sessions is influenced by the social and cultural contexts of the program. The topics and practices that are valued by the program and critical to its mission are reflected in the program's training plan. Training sessions and techniques can enhance the program's climate through activities such as team-building. Trainers should consider how trainees' cultures may affect their behavior during training sessions.

As human beings, we are influenced by the culture we live in; it affects our behavior, reactions, values, experiences, and perceptions. Trainees bring these cultural influences to the training environment. Consider the following influences, which can affect group behavior and training situations.

The Role of the Teacher as an Authority Figure

For members of some cultural groups, the trainer or teacher holds a special position and is considered an authority figure. Individuals who hold this view may be reluctant to challenge the trainer's point of view or question her information. In some cases, some participants may even expect that the trainer, as an authority, should provide all the answers to any challenges experienced by the group. Participants with this orientation may have difficulty participating in group work or activities in which the trainees must find their own solutions to challenges.

Experience versus Education

Some cultures honor life experience. Other cultures honor educational attainment. Always start off a session with a new group by introducing yourself *briefly* and providing your education and experience credentials. Whenever possible, take a few minutes to understand the education and experience levels of individuals in the group. Doing so will help you recognize the experts in your group and use their wisdom as a resource for the group's benefit.

Risk-Taking Behavior

Learning new skills can involve taking risks. Trainees risk embarrassment when they practice new skills in a group. They may also take risks to complete team-building or training activities that involve competition or physical or mental challenges. Trainees from some cultural groups may be extremely uncomfortable participating in activities that require risk. Activities involving potential embarrassment or rewarding weaknesses may also be objectionable for some participants. Remember that adult learners commonly resist activities that might reveal weaknesses or cause them to feel humiliated in any way. Allow opportunities for participants to practice individually before sharing with others whenever possible. At the very least, limit activities that could potentially involve risk or humiliation to pairs or very small groups. Allow participants to opt out of these activities if they choose.

Language

Language is at the very heart of a culture. Not only may trainees of differing cultures speak different languages; they may use the same language in different ways. As the trainer of a group, you should expect different cultures and language use among any group of trainees. Be prepared to offer explanations for slang terms or technical jargon. Be particularly cautious about using abbreviations or acronyms. Never assume that all trainees are familiar with the same terms—even terms common to the early childhood profession.

Humor is something else that is culturally specific. Jokes, riddles, and even humorous comments can be troublesome. Humor can be challenging for members of certain cultural groups when they do not understand the references in jokes. These trainees may feel ostracized because they are not able to join in the fun. Humor can also be challenging in cases when members of a cultural group are offended by a reference that is intended to be humorous.

Topics that may be funny to some trainees can be offensive to others. This does not mean humor is entirely off limits for trainers—simply exercise caution and choose only humorous references or jokes that stay far from any political, religious, or "adult" content.

Improving the Social Climate during Training Sessions

Danielle quickly scribbled notes on the pad in front of her. She was inspired by her observation of the group time in Malena's classroom. "The children were so engrossed in the conversation," she wrote. "If only our conversations during training sessions could be that animated. Malena really has a knack at drawing in the children—I can learn from that."

One of the final social and cultural considerations for trainers is their responsibility to create and maintain a pleasant social atmosphere during training sessions. As the facilitator of the training session, you must use your skills and knowledge to design the session so that participants feel welcomed and valued. Embracing the adult learning principles discussed in chapter 2 will help you create a supportive climate for your training sessions. Implementing the following simple and practical suggestions will also enhance your efforts.

Use Participants' Names

Using a person's name is a gesture of respect and promotes feelings of comfort and belonging. Interestingly, participants tend to view trainers who use their names frequently as well-prepared and engaged.

Be Careful about Your Body Language

As a trainer, you convey powerful messages verbally and nonverbally. You must be extremely careful about what you say, and you need to be equally careful about the messages you send with your posture, gestures, eye contact, and body positions. To create a welcoming environment for trainees, avoid crossing your arms, turning your back to participants who are speaking, and withholding eye contact. These gestures indicate to participants that you are uninterested in what they have to say. Conversely, use eye contact, a nod of the head, or a smile to give confidence to reluctant participants.

Ask Open-Ended Questions

Open-ended questions do not lend themselves to yes or no answers. An example of an open-ended question is "How do you encourage creativity among children?" A closed question is "Do you encourage creativity among children?"

Open-ended questions are valuable tools for creating a positive training environment because they encourage participation and demonstrate to trainees that you value their knowledge, experience, and contributions. Open-ended questions provide better insight into trainees' learning. Listen carefully to their answers to gauge their understanding of the concepts or skills you have introduced.

Invite Questions from Participants

While asking questions of the participants is important, inviting questions *from* the participants is equally essential in creating a positive tone. No matter how many times adults are reminded that there are no bad questions, they are still reluctant to ask for fear of appearing silly, resistant, or slow to master content. By frequently inviting questions, you remind participants that you expect them and that they are valued and helpful to everyone's learning. You can ask "Who has a question?" or "What questions would help to clarify this topic?" to demonstrate that you expect questions and that knowledgeable participants offer questions to help the group learn together.

Frequently Acknowledge Participation and Effort

Like children, adults respond to acknowledgment and praise. Provide specific, positive comments to trainees who demonstrate effort, take risks, or make progress during training. The following responses can be used to acknowledge trainees' contributions:

- "Interesting plan."
- "Great focus on that idea."

- "You're really showing creativity."
- "That's a great idea; let's explore that some more."
- "Good question. Who has a suggestion to offer in response?"
- "Nice effort; you're making progress on this."

When planning for the social and cultural environments of the training session, what you do and don't do make a difference to your trainees. Use your common sense and consider the type of environment in which you would feel comfortable as a trainee. Employing these simple ideas will greatly enhance the experience your trainees enjoy and the knowledge and skills they acquire.

Summary

All human beings are influenced by the social and cultural contexts in which they live and work. The program's culture influences how training is conducted, if training is valued, how it is organized, and the social goals that may be developed for training sessions.

Training can be used to influence the social environment of the program. Teamwork and communication are essential for any program to function smoothly, and these can be influenced by training. Many training programs include ice-breakers or team-building activities as best practices to improve networking and build communication and collegiality among teachers.

Trainers have a variety of responsibilities when facilitating training sessions. They should respond to the cultural differences among trainees and should use a variety of techniques to sustain a positive social and learning environment.

Designing and Implementing Training

CHAPTER **6** Training Analysis and Design

Rhea shuffled through the file drawer looking for the handouts for this evening's training session. "I know I saved those handouts! Where could I have put them?" Finally locating the missing papers, Rhea thought, "Now, what should I say about these?"

Once you have identified the broad themes that shape the training in your program—compliance needs, stages of teacher development, program training needs, and social needs—it is time to begin developing the training materials you will use to meet the teachers' needs. You will use the information that you have gathered so far about their needs and those of your program.

In some cases, you will create materials for use with a group of teachers. In other cases, you may create materials that will be used by only one or two teachers at a time. Just as in developing curriculum for early childhood classrooms, developing

training materials for adult learning follows a specific process and uses well-defined techniques.

Training Materials: Buy or Build?

Before you begin developing training materials, you should consider whether the materials you need are already commercially available. Many organizations and publishers in the early childhood industry sell prepared training materials for use by early childhood programs. In some cases, these materials may be exactly what you need. Using prepared materials can save time and provide you with a model to use when developing your own materials.

While purchasing prepared training materials can save time, you should also consider its disadvantages. If the objectives and content of the training materials do not match your needs, you can spend as much time adapting them as you might spend creating exactly what you need. Using training materials that do not completely meet the needs of your teachers wastes valuable training time and program resources. To fully appreciate the potential match between your needs and the materials you are considering, review the following elements:

- Training objectives. Match the objectives that the materials address with your own needs.
- Intended audience. Prepared materials often describe the audience for whom the materials were developed. It is worth considering whether the materials were designed for experienced or novice teachers.
- Language and tone. Does the language of the training materials fit the culture and sensibilities of your program? Ask yourself if the information sounds as though it belongs to your program.
- Activities and examples. Read all of the activities and decide if they ring true for your program. If role-playing activities or case studies are used, do they reflect your program in ways that will make them meaningful learning experiences?

The questions on the form that follows will help you determine if it is worthwhile to purchase prepared training materials. Carefully examine any items to which you answer no. These items present obstacles that will need to be overcome if you use

prepared materials for your training sessions. For a reproducible copy of Evaluating Training Materials for Purchase, see form 12 in the appendix.

A Word about Copyright Limitations

Once you have decided to purchase training materials for your use, be sure you are absolutely clear about any limits associated with the materials. Some training programs allow unlimited copies and multiple uses; others do not. You are responsible for complying with the copyright limitations of any materials you purchase. Never assume that purchasing training materials gives you unlimited rights to copy, use, or alter these training materials.

Be aware that commercial copy and printing shops may not be willing to reproduce handouts that are marked with a copyright other than your own. If you plan to have copies made at a copy shop, be sure you have evidence that you are legally permitted to copy the materials.

The ADDIE Model

Often you will decide to develop training materials for your own use as a trainer. Sometimes you may also develop training materials that will be used by other trainers. In either case, it is essential to follow a carefully constructed process for the design

Evaluating Training Materials for Purchase

Answer each question by circling YES or NO. Carefully consider any items that you mark NO.

Do the objectives of the materials match your program's needs?	YES	NO
Do the activities and examples fit the program?	YES	NO
Can the materials be used with very little adaptation?	YES	NO
Can the materials be copied to meet your needs?	YES	NO
Is the source of the material credible?	YES	NO
Is the material of a quality you will be proud to use?	YES	NO
Can any parts of the training materials that do not meet your needs be eliminated?	YES	NO
Are the materials easy to read, logically ordered, and sufficiently detailed?	YES	NO
Does the cost of the materials fit within your budget?	YES	NO
Is the expense of the training materials a good value?	YES	NO

Spotlight on the ADDIE Model

The ADDIE model represents the most commonly used method for developing training materials for use with adult learners. The ADDIE model can be represented as a circular design or a series of sequential steps. Either way the model is depicted, its major steps produce training materials that effectively meet adults' needs and support development of skills, knowledge, and changes in attitudes.

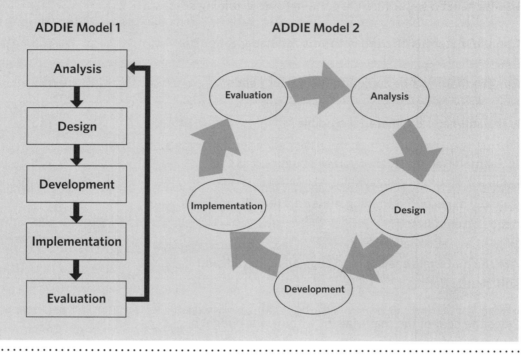

and development of those materials. Doing so will help ensure that the results of your training meet the needs of the teachers you support. From this point forward, we will focus primarily on training materials used in instructor-led training because those used in individual training or coaching do not always use the same instructional design models.

Instructional design of adult training materials can be accomplished in many different ways. As in constructing curriculum for young children, instructional designers can choose from many different models for their work. The most commonly used model for instructional design of adult training materials is ADDIE. ADDIE is the acronym for Analysis, Design,

Development, Implementation, and Evaluation. Throughout the remaining chapters of this book, we will explore each step in the ADDIE instructional design model. You will see how the steps link together to create a plan for a training session. Using the forms provided, you can practice each step and develop your own training sessions.

Analysis

Lavonne reviewed the results from the training questionnaire. She was surprised to see how many of her teachers wanted more training on child guidance. "It seems as though we talk about guidance all the time. I wonder what else they need to know."

Before beginning the actual construction of training materials, you need to be sure you have adequately defined the training needs of the group. Some trainers are tempted to bypass this step. They assume that because the decision to conduct training has been made, no further analysis is needed. In reality, an appropriate amount of analysis, conducted after the decision to train has been made, contributes significantly to the success of the training.

In prior chapters, we have discussed some of the work trainers do to identify training needs involving compliance requirements, program goals, and individual needs of teachers. Once you have established the areas for training, analyze the specific learning objectives for each training session and strive to completely understand trainees' current knowledge and skills and what knowledge and skills are required by the program. In this step, your goal is to determine

- the exact content of the training that will address the need.
- the extent of the change in behavior that will be expected of the trainees.
- the characteristics of the audience for the training.
- the training environment.
- any special considerations that will affect the training.

Content

During your analysis, you must make a number of decisions about what to include and what to exclude in the training. One of the most common errors trainers make is to try to tackle too much content in a single session. Narrowing the focus is critical during the development process.

Remember, at this stage in the instructional design, your general training topic has already been determined. Your goal now is to understand any gaps between the teachers' current level of knowledge and skills and the desired on-the-job behavior to be presented in the training session. If your analysis during this planning phase uncovers additional training topics or needs, note that information for future development but do not try to incorporate additional or unrelated topics into this training session.

The assessment techniques described in chapter 4 can be used to analyze and understand the individual needs of teachers as you develop the training. The chart that follows describes the techniques for assessing the training needs that are available. Choose one or two of the methods listed to gather information about the specific needs of your trainees. You should also use the analysis techniques to gather information about your audience's characteristics, the changes in the behavior of the trainees that will be introduced in the training, and the training environment. Each of these topics is addressed in sections that follow the chart. Do not attempt to use all of these techniques each time you develop a training, or your analysis will simply absorb much of your planning time.

METHOD	DESCRIPTION OF USE
Interviews	Interviews are an excellent way to gather information about specific training needs. At this stage, your brief interviews should focus solely on the training topic under development. All teachers in a program do not need to be interviewed during your training needs analysis; a sampling can be selected for interviews to save time.
Performance appraisals	Finding commonalities in the performance appraisals of a group of teachers can yield useful information. Teachers who share the same development needs (as indicated by their performance appraisals) are candidates for group training experiences. Analyzing performance appraisals can help you define the right audience for the training you are preparing. Performance appraisals may also help identify teachers who would be good candidates for interviews or observations.
Observations	Observations may be the best way to fully understand teachers' training needs. Although observations can be time consuming, they provide useful pictures of the teachers' current skills and knowledge. Observations also provide insight into teachers' preferences and openness to change. This information can provide the defining difference between an ordinary training session and one that meets the particular needs of a group of teachers.
Surveys and questionnaires	Surveys or questionnaires can gather a pertinent amount of information very quickly. Because a general training topic has already been selected, surveys or questionnaires can be used to fine-tune the content or to understand the depth of the teachers' training needs. An example of a training needs assessment survey is found on page 88.

METHOD	DESCRIPTION OF USE
Data	Analyzing data can be useful for understanding training needs across the program. Data can tell you about the frequency of injuries or incidents, enrollment trends, test scores, or other information about the program. As you consider data, remember that alone they rarely tell the entire story of an employee's performance. Combining them with other needs assessment techniques, such as interviews or observations, gives a more complete evaluation.

These techniques will help you make accurate decisions about the content of your training sessions.

The survey on page 88 demonstrates how data about a single training subject can be collected. Because the training topic—in this case, family-style meal service—has already been defined, the survey can focus on a narrower set of questions. Use the Training Session Planner on page 93 to capture the findings from your own analysis.

Change Management

Creating change is an important part of any training session. Remember, the goal of most training is to change on-the-job behavior. Trainers should know trainees are likely to view the desired change as challenging or relatively easy. While some adults adapt to new behaviors with relative ease, others find almost any kind of change difficult.

You should assess the degree of change inherent in the training topic and how much attention you will need to direct to it in your session. Review the needs assessment information you have collected through interviews, observations, surveys, and other means. As you review this information, remember that failing to address change management violates some important principles of adult learning introduced in chapters 2 and 3. Understanding the extent to which you are asking adults to change their skills or behaviors is part of honoring their experiences and readiness as learners. You may find some helpful information to guide you in this area by reviewing Putting Andragogy to Work on page 41.

The Change Management Questionnaire on page 89 provides a series of questions to help you understand how your trainees react to change. Use your own knowledge of the trainees, or plan time to conduct a few short interviews to gather information. For a reproducible copy of Change Management Questionnaire, see form 14 in the appendix.

Training Survey: Family-Style Meal Service

The topic for our teacher training session next month will be Family-Style Meal Service. We have identified this practice as an opportunity to enhance our program and to move closer to meeting accreditation criteria. Please complete the following questionnaire to help us create the training session that will best meet your needs and facilitate a smooth transition to this new practice.

Please circle the response that best matches your point of view. Write any additional comments in the space provided.

YES   NO   I am familiar with the concepts underlying the use of family-style meal service.

YES   NO   I am using or have used family-style meal service in my classroom.
If YES, how would you describe those experiences?

_____

_____

_____

YES   NO   I am excited about the idea of trying family-style meal service in my classroom. Please explain why or why not.

_____

_____

_____

What challenges, if any, do you anticipate as we implement family-style meal service?

_____

_____

_____

Thank you for your thoughtful contributions!

Change Management Questionnaire

· ·

1. How great is the difference between the desired behavior and the current behavior? How much do teachers need to change their on-the-job behaviors or routines to be consistent with the training session's objectives?

2. Which teachers, if any, are already using the desired skills or behaviors? Will these teachers be willing to speak on behalf of the desired or new behaviors during the training sessions? Are the teachers using the desired behaviors considered leaders among the group?

3. Are some parts of the content more challenging than others? Can the more challenging parts of the content be introduced after the more agreeable content has been addressed and the group is working productively?

4. How do the teachers in this group respond to changes in ways of doing things? Are most open to change in general? Is change infrequent or frequent? Have changes in the past been implemented smoothly or only with significant challenges?

5. What are the possible challenges that teachers face when implementing the new behaviors or skills introduced in the training? Are these challenges manageable? Are the solutions to the challenges within the teachers' control?

6. What are the benefits of implementing new ideas, skills, or behaviors to teachers? What are the benefits to children? Do changes make the teachers' days more manageable or enjoyable?

7. If you have worked with this group of trainees before, in what ways do they usually resist change? Are they vocal about their misgivings? Do they challenge new ideas immediately or wait until the trainer solicits feedback?

The answers to the questions in the Change Management Questionnaire will not necessarily change the content or direction of your training session. They will, however, help you think about your presentation, the expectations of the group, and the extent to which you may need to distribute time on different aspects of the session. For example, if you determine that several teachers are more open to change than the rest of the group or have even tried some of the ideas you will be presenting, you may decide to involve these change champions as leaders of small discussion groups. Knowing this may influence how you organize smaller groups and what topics the trainer will discuss.

Characteristics of the Audience

Understanding as much as possible about the participants in the training you are developing will increase the likelihood that your efforts will be successful. If you are the supervisor of the teachers who will participate in the training, you may already know a great deal about their characteristics and habits as trainees. If you are not familiar with them, you should spend a few minutes discussing them with someone who knows them well. Consider asking all or some of the following questions:

- What is the typical attitude among the group about training sessions?
- What kinds of activities have worked well with this group in the past? What

kinds of activities have not worked well? Why?
- Is the session for teachers who work with a particular age group or a variety of age groups? What age groups of children do these teachers work with?
- How long has this group worked together? What is the general level of education and experience among the group?
- Have any recent events affected the group that could be relevant to the training topic?
- Do any participants have special needs? What accommodations should you be prepared to make?

Sometimes you may be asked to prepare training materials or sessions with little or no knowledge of who will participate. This may happen if you prepare a training session for a conference or local professional group. In such cases, you can only make a few basic assumptions about your trainees: they have an interest in the topic and they belong to the group for which the conference or association was designed.

One best practice that trainers often use is to craft the session's title to appeal to teachers with particular characteristics. For example A Look at Emergent Curriculum for Master Teachers describes a session intended to attract more veteran teachers and those with a predisposition toward emergent curriculum. Some conferences or association meetings allow trainers to designate the types of teachers their sessions are designed for. Sessions may be designated for novice or experienced teachers or may be divided by the age group of children that teachers work with. If such segmented training is an option, think carefully about the breadth of the audience you wish to address in a single training session. While it is tempting to try to appeal to all types of teachers and attract the widest possible audience, it is also very challenging to meet the needs of a very diverse group of teachers in one session.

Record what you have learned about your trainees on the Training Session Planner on page 93.

Training Environment

Joya looked around the conference room. She was surprised to see fifty chairs in the room but no tables. Joya looked quickly at her notes. She told her training partner, "We'll need to change the group work. Without small tables, we'll need a different activity. Any ideas?"

Trainees affect a training session's characteristics and objectives. Similarly, the environment in which the training will be presented affects the design and delivery of your material. For instance, you may find that some activities are very effective when used in small groups of trainees but are very ineffective in large groups.

If you have ever tried to use the same training materials in a wide variety of situations, no doubt you have discovered that modifications were needed to meet the trainees' needs. Perhaps you changed the amount of time allotted for activities to accommodate a larger group or reduced the amount of active movement in a small room to accommodate trainees. In both cases, the impact that environment can have on the design and delivery of a training session is notable. Collecting the following information about the physical environment in which you hold the training will help you make wise design decisions:

- number of trainees
- size of space
- room set-up and furnishings (tables, chairs, microphone, presenter's podium, etc.)
- time of day and duration of training
- space challenges or limits (noise level, visual obstructions, lighting, etc.)
- restrictions on audio/visual devices (availability of electricity, screens to show visuals, inability to dim the room, etc.)

Sometimes you will have control over the training environment. You may possess or can request ideal furnishings, audio/visual support, size of space, and so on. As you design and develop the training session and materials, make note of any special environmental considerations the session requires. This will save time during your last-minute preparations.

Use the Training Session Planner on page 93 to note pertinent environmental considerations.

Special Considerations for Training Events

Inevitably, once you believe your analysis has accounted for every possible consideration, something else pops up. Now you have the opportunity to demonstrate your flexibility and creativity as a trainer. If your session is part of a larger training event, some special considerations can be predicted with a few well-chosen questions to the person organizing the training session. Consider asking the following questions:

- Is there a theme or organizing slogan to the training that might influence the title or content of my training session?
- Are there any other events or sessions before or after my session that could affect the tone of the day, the enthusiasm of the group, or acceptance of the content by trainees?
- Are there any other training sessions at the same time or immediately before or after mine presenting a different point of view?

One of the biggest challenges to designing any training session is the amount of time you have with your trainees. Whether you are creating a training session for your own program or one to present at a conference or for another group, the session can be affected by unexpected variables—weather, food delays, late participants, other trainers who run over their allotted time. Therefore, it is wise to build flexibility into your session. This topic will be addressed in more detail in subsequent sections.

Turn to the Training Session Planner on page 93 to note any special considerations of which you have become aware. For a reproducible copy of the Training Session Planner, see form 15 in the appendix.

Now that you have analyzed the needs of your trainees and your training session circumstances, you are ready to begin designing the training session and materials. At this point in your instructional design, you should have a well-developed idea about what you hope to accomplish. To test this, close your eyes and picture your trainees demonstrating the teaching skills, behaviors, or knowledge that are the subject of the training session. If you can envision the desired result of your training, you are ready to move on to design the learning objectives and the actual training session.

Design

"Two textbooks, four journal articles, eight pages of notes," Sheila muttered to herself. "How will I ever cover all of this in one training session?" She flipped through a few pages of

Training Session Planner

Topic _____

Details of training session (if known)

Date _____ Time _____

Location _____

General description of content to be addressed

_____

_____

Change management considerations

_____

_____

Training audience—who, experience, diversity, special needs

_____

_____

Training environment—where will training take place, furnishings, equipment, etc.

_____

_____

Special considerations (if any)

_____

_____

_____

the first journal article. Suddenly the answer occurred to her: "I need to get organized. I have to pick the most important things."

During the design phase of training development, you must hone your general ideas about learning objectives and specific content. Many trainers consider this phase the most difficult because selectivity and specificity are critical to success.

Learning Objectives

The first step in the design process is to reduce the content to a small number of concrete learning objectives. The learning objectives make clear what will and will not be addressed in the session. They specify what the trainees' behavior should look like after the training. They answer the questions who? what? when? and how well? Most trainers use a simple formula to write learning objectives:

_____ will _____ , by _____ , _____ .
(Who)   (what)   (when)   (how well)

The following learning objectives are based on this formula:

All teachers will use family-style meal service by next Tuesday for each meal and snack.
   (who)   (what)   (when)   (how well)

Preschool teachers will plan developmentally appropriate outdoor activities by next week
   (who)   (what)   (when)
and will be able to do so 100% of the time.
            (how well)

All teachers will be able to complete the new attendance form by the end of the session
   (who)   (what)   (when)
and will be able to do so each day beginning next week.
            (how well)

These learning objectives would be addressed in three different training sessions. Most individual training sessions have two or three *related* learning objectives. Learning objectives are constructed by considering your ultimate goals for the training session. They constitute the most important focus of the training session and define the outcomes you are expecting. Each learning objective should help to answer this question: What do I want the trainees to be able to do as a result of participating in this training session? For example, the training session on family-style meal service might focus on these three related learning objectives:

- All teachers will use family style meal service by next Tuesday for each meal and snack.
- All teachers will be able to comfortably discuss family-style meal service with families, including discussion of its benefits for young children, beginning next Tuesday.
- All teachers will consistently address child guidance issues that may arise during family-style meals and snacks with positive guidance and developmental techniques, as described in the training session, beginning next Tuesday.

If you are unable to describe the session in two or three objectives, consider reducing the content you are considering. Sessions that can only be described in many learning objectives probably offer too much content. If all of the content you have described in your learning objectives is essential for your trainees' success, consider expanding your training to include several sessions over a longer period of time. Use the form that follows to write learning objectives for a training session you are planning. For a reproducible copy of Identifying Objectives, see form 16 in the appendix.

Organizing Content

Now that you have identified the learning objectives for your training topic, you can begin to organize the content. Trainers use many techniques to define specific content. One technique that most early childhood professionals are familiar with is webbing. Many of you have probably used webbing to develop curriculum for young children.

Webbing is a visual tool used to depict the content. It and similar techniques allow you to organize your thoughts about a topic before you begin to write down the actual training activities and materials that will make up the training session. Using a technique such as webbing helps ensure that the materials you develop are orderly and logical. Webbing may also help point you toward a particular design for your training session, a topic we will discuss later.

To begin webbing, identify the central idea you are addressing in your training session. From that central idea, you then identify subtopics and the concepts related

Identifying Objectives

· ·

Topic _____

Details of training session (if known)

Date _____   Time _____

Location _____

Write a general description of content to be addressed.

_____

_____

_____

_____

Create two or three learning objectives for your training session. Remember, your learning objectives should answer the questions who? what? when? and how well?

1. _____

_____

_____

_____

2. _____

_____

_____

_____

3. _____

_____

_____

_____

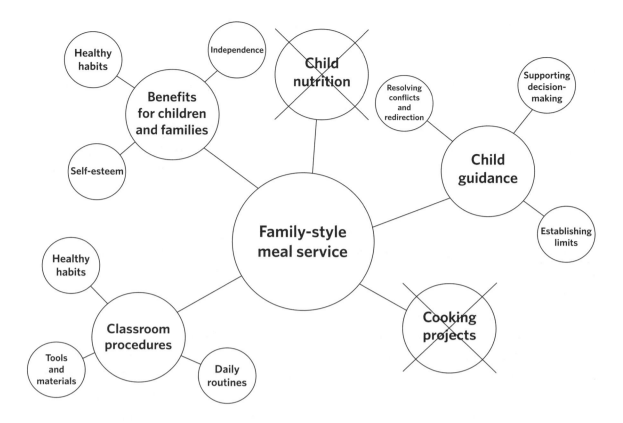

to each. The learning objectives you have identified will guide you in developing your subtopics. The illustration above depicts a webbing activity about family-style meal service.

Notice as you review this web that the central idea—family-style meal service—is indicated in the center circle. Five subtopics have been identified: child nutrition, benefits for children and families, classroom procedures, cooking projects, and child guidance. There is no special rule that limits the number of subtopics; you may have more subtopics or fewer depending upon the central idea you are exploring. After reviewing your web, however, you may need to eliminate some of the subtopics based on the priorities of your session and the amount of time you have available. For example, in creating the web for family-style meal service, the trainer listed the subtopics of child nutrition and cooking projects. These original ideas were eliminated in order to keep the training within the time allocated and to allow for deep discussion and mastery on the primary subjects identified in the learning objectives. After settling on three subtopics, the trainer added several ideas related to each one.

Striking a perfect balance between thoroughly covering an important topic and overwhelming trainees with too much information is one of the biggest challenges for trainers. Success in this area comes with practice and thoughtful consideration. A good training session covers a few ideas completely and allows trainees to master the content. Trainees leave such sessions feeling successful and ready to apply what they have learned. A good rule of thumb is to include no more than three new ideas in any one training session. This is almost always preferable to covering a greater quantity of material but leaving the session with questions unanswered or skills not mastered. Sessions that take the broad approach can leave trainees overwhelmed, confused, unsure, and unprepared for the challenges of implementing new skills.

Use the basic webbing technique in the space on the next page to begin developing your training session. Write the central idea in the middle circle. Then identify a few subtopics related to the central idea and some of the smaller ideas related to each subtopic. Refer to the learning objectives you have already created. Check your content to be certain your learning objectives are adequately addressed. Add additional circles as needed to capture the content for your training session. At this point, eliminate ideas that are clearly not going to fit with the rest of your content or address your learning objectives. For a reproducible copy of Webbing a Training Topic, see form 17 in the appendix.

Training Designs

Six training designs are commonly used. Your content is likely to fit in one or two of these designs. Some content is an obvious fit for one of the training designs, while other content can fit within a number of possible designs. As you review each of the designs, consider which one may best fit the training content you are developing.

Chronological Order

This design introduces content that follows a time line. For example, history topics are almost always introduced in chronological order. A trainer might use chronological order to introduce the order of events for a field trip or a special event.

Procedural Order

This design is similar to chronological order but introduces the steps in a process. In this case, the steps are not necessarily time bound, as they are in chronological order, but they do have an implied order. Trainers use procedural order to introduce topics such as the steps in conducting a family conference or those in completing a form. Procedural order is frequently used as the design for at least part of a training session.

Webbing a Training Topic

· ·

Topic _____

Identify the central idea of the training topic in the middle circle. Then identify a few subtopics related to the central idea and some of the smaller ideas related to each subtopic. Use the session's learning objectives to guide the development of your topics. Add additional circles to the web as needed to capture the content for the training session.

It is often paired with other designs to fully introduce content that includes but is not limited to a procedure.

Problem to Solution

This design is frequently used in sessions devoted to problem resolution or improving quality or performance. For example, this design could be used in a session in which participants are introduced to the problem of children's challenging behaviors during group times. Several potential solutions are then presented and discussed. Sessions using this design are often highly interactive and rely on trainees' active participation in discussing choices from among potential solutions.

General to Specific

This commonly used design is appropriate to training situations in which one broad topic and several related subtopics are addressed. For example, in a session on literacy, the general topic of literacy in early childhood would be introduced and specific subtopics, such as reading aloud or alphabetic principle, would be introduced to support the general topic by adding detail and context.

This design is often used in combination with other designs, especially procedural design. For example, a session covering wellness practices might use this design by introducing the general benefits of and premises for promoting wellness among children. Then a procedural design might be used to introduce some specific procedures for hand washing and diapering.

Simple to Complex

This design is often used when the trainer anticipates reluctance or resistance from trainees. Introducing simple concepts first allows trainees to warm to new ideas and builds their confidence. After they have mastered the simple ideas, they can to move on to more complex ones.

An example of a training session using this design addresses child guidance techniques. The session would begin with simple situations that have obvious solutions. As trainees develop confidence, more complex situations would be introduced, requiring trainees to apply what they have learned in novel ways and with increasing competence.

Known to Unknown

This design is consistent with the belief that adults learn best when new information builds upon existing knowledge. In early childhood education, this idea is often referred to as activating prior knowledge. Sessions using this design begin with a summary of existing practices or information that is already well-known and used by the trainees. Beginning with familiar topics builds the confidence of the trainees and increases their interest in new topics.

A session using this design could begin with a general topic that is well-known to the trainees. For example, the trainer might begin with an overview of the development of typical three year olds. Using this information as a foundation, the trainer then might introduce an unknown topic such as a new curriculum to be used in the program for three-year-olds.

Most training sessions use one or perhaps two of these training designs. Review the webbing you completed for your training session. Does the session clearly fit within one of these designs? Could more than one of the designs be used to address the content of your session? Choose the design that best fits the learning objectives you have created and the content you are addressing. Make a few notes to indicate how you can organize the content based on the design or designs you have chosen.

The training designs described here and the learning objectives identified for a training on family-style meal service yield the following outline.

Example

Session Topic: Family-Style Meal Service

Part 1: Overview of the benefits to children and families of family-style meal service (general-to-specific design)

Address the following learning objectives:

- All teachers will be able to comfortably discuss family-style meal service with families, including a discussion of its benefits for young children, beginning next Tuesday.
- All teachers will consistently address child guidance issues that may arise during family-style meal service with positive guidance and developmental techniques, as described in the training session during meals and snacks, by next Tuesday.

Part 2: Process and procedure for introducing and using family-style meal service (procedural design)

Addresses the following learning objectives:

- All teachers will use family-style meal service by next Tuesday for each meal and snack.
- All teachers will consistently address child guidance issues that may arise during family-style meal service with positive guidance and developmental techniques, as described in the training session during meals and snacks, by next Tuesday.

Summary

The ADDIE instructional design model provides a specific, easy-to-follow procedure for analyzing, designing, developing, implementing, and evaluating training sessions and materials. As part of the ADDIE procedure, trainers analyze the content and change management necessary to address the training needs of a specific audience in a specific environment. A variety of analysis techniques are available to trainers to hone the training content.

The overall design of a training session is dependent upon the learning objectives. Trainers carefully describe the objectives of the training session to provide focus for the content. Identifying the content related to each learning objective leads the trainer to a training design. Thoughtful development of learning objectives and careful definition of objective-related content are critical to successful planning of training sessions.

CHAPTER 7

Development of Training Sessions and Materials

Fawn looked at the learning objectives for her training session. "The procedure I am teaching is pretty clear. But I hate training sessions that are just boring lectures filled with do's and don'ts. How can I make this session more interesting?" Chelsea looked up from the paperwork on her desk. "How about a game? Everyone likes games, right?"

After the needs of the trainees have been assessed and the learning objectives and overall design determined, it is time to develop the training activities and materials that will bring the session to life. During this stage of the instructional design, trainers exercise their creativity and employ many of the same skills you use in the classroom when working with young children. As you develop your training session, think about the approaches you used when planning a group time for children in your classroom. As a teacher, you incorporate

specific learning objectives in your teaching, use a variety of activities and teaching methods to introduce and practice skills, and observe the children's interactions and activities to check for mastery. In addition to these fundamentals, you probably use attention-grabbers, fun, and routines to organize learning activities within a group time. As a trainer, you will use very similar techniques as you develop training sessions and materials. Organize your training sessions into three major parts: the introduction, the body of the presentations, and the closing or wrap-up.

Introducing the Session

Every training session has to start somewhere. As the old adage goes, you never get a second chance to make a first impression. In addition to making that positive first impression, the introduction has a number of important functions. First, it captures the attention of the trainees. It is not unusual for training sessions to be held at the end of the day or in the midst of other activities like staff meetings. The introduction separates the training session from activities that have preceded it and signals the trainees to mentally shift into learning mode.

The introduction is also the right time to address any of the important housekeeping details associated with a training session. Besides providing an overview of the agenda, the introduction addresses logistical items such as breaks, refreshments, attendance taking, and so on. Addressing these items early in the session is important because doing so relieves trainees from wondering about them later. One important detail is introducing yourself as the trainer. Unless you are known to all of the trainees, take a few minutes to give a brief explanation of your interest in and expertise on the topic.

Often trainers use the introduction as a time to offer an ice-breaker or team-builder or to allow trainees to introduce themselves. Ice-breakers and team-builders can serve an important social function within the training session; designed properly, they can introduce the training's content in an enjoyable, energizing way. But they may not be good choices for every training session. Refer to chapter 5 for more information on the benefits and challenges associated with these interactive social tools.

Finally, the most important function of the introduction is to address the training's content and the expectations of trainees. Trainers should present the session's learning objectives and explain to trainees how they will benefit from the content. This is your chance to address the learners' need to know, as described in the section on andragogy. Refer to the Putting Andragogy to Work worksheet on page 44 for ideas you can incorporate into your introduction. For a reproducible copy of Develop Your Introduction, see form 18 in the appendix.

The Body of the Session: Addressing the Content

During the body of the presentation, trainers use a variety of techniques and activities to engage trainees with the content. It is here that the learning objectives are met. The trainer must also ensure that training content transfers to on-the job behavior and assess the trainees' mastery of the objectives.

Most of your training session is devoted to introducing, practicing, and mastering content. To craft the body of the session, refer to the design decisions you have already made. Your design choices—procedural, chronological, and so on—will determine the logical order in which you introduce content.

One of the common mistakes made by trainers is to assume that they must present

Develop Your Introduction

· ·

Topic _____

Details of training session (if known)

Date _____   Time _____

Location _____

General description of content to be addressed _____

_____

_____

Develop a plan for the introduction to your training session. Use the following short checklist to ensure that you have addressed all of the important elements found in an introduction.

☐ Attention-getting opener
☐ Trainer's introduction
☐ Overview of agenda and logistics details
☐ Ice-breaker or team-builder (if appropriate)
☐ Explanation of the learning objectives and trainees' need to know

Brief overview of the introduction _____

_____

_____

_____

_____

_____

_____

_____

all of the content themselves. Bias toward lecture or similar trainer-led presentations is sometimes based on the teaching methods we experienced in college or other adult learning environments. Adults benefit from a wide range of presentation techniques and often learn best from more interactive techniques and methods. The following broad categories are among those most frequently used in training sessions.

Lecture or Presentation

Although lecturing should not be the sole method used in training sessions, it is one of the most common ways in which information can be presented. Use these best practices:

- Use lecture only when other, more interactive, techniques are not practical options.
- Use lecture when information must be communicated in a very specific way.
- Use lecture to convey information to large groups whenever activities or trainee participation would be impossible to manage.
- Keep lectures short, and pair them with activities that involve trainees.
- A lecture may be particularly appropriate when a guest speaker or well-known expert is presenting information as part of the training session.

When you use a lecture or presentation, increase its effectiveness by including handouts, visual aids such as charts or slide shows, occasional discussion topics, table work in small groups, and question-and-answer sessions.

Demonstrations

Demonstrations are an excellent way to bolster learning opportunities in your training session. They are especially effective for teaching skills and modeling the use of particular tools, procedures, or processes for trainees. As you plan for demonstrations, incorporate the following best practices:

- Use the actual tools or materials that will be used by the trainees whenever possible.
- Demonstrate the process or procedure so it approximates the way in which trainees will be expected to use it on the job.
- Incorporate visual aids with verbal directions during demonstrations.
- Practice demonstrations several times before the training session to be sure that all materials, processes, and procedures are completely ready and you feel comfortable modeling the behavior you want trainees to demonstrate on the job.
- Allow enough time for the demonstration; rushing will not result in the desired learning and can frustrate participants.

Demonstrations can be a powerful learning device and add variety and interest for adult learners. As a trainer, you must plan and practice your demonstrations thoughtfully. Offering yourself as a role model for a procedure or process can be stressful, but it also enhances your credibility.

Activities

Trainers use a variety of activities to engage trainees in the learning experience. These can include games, role-playing, simulations, skits, artwork, journaling, and other experiences. Activities are useful because they encourage trainees to learn by doing. Some activities enhance learning by modeling the way in which the training will be used on the job. Role-playing is one example of a training activity that simulates on-the-job behavior. Activities within the training session to provide motivation and to energize trainees are also useful. Experienced trainers use the following best practices when considering activities within the instructional design:

- Use activities to support the learning objectives. Resist the temptation to use activities simply because they are fun or appeal to trainees.
- Allow adequate time for the activities you have planned. Incorporate time for directions, creating groups, completing the activity, discussing the results of the activity, and making the transition to the next part of the training session.
- Consider the social and cultural needs of participants as you choose activities.

- Be selective about the use of activities for very large groups. Moving large numbers of trainees to and from activities can be very challenging and requires a fair amount of skill from the trainer.
- Plan activities that can be performed in the room or area where the training will be conducted. For example, small group activities work best at tables of six to eight participants in the meeting room.

As you consider activities to include in your training session, think about the activities in relation to the trainees. Some audiences like dramatic activities; others do not. Some audiences enjoy competitive activities; others do not.

Discussions or Problem Solving

Many training sessions use large- or small-group discussions to introduce information, solve problems, create change, and plan actions to implement the training content on the job. Discussions are especially useful to activate adult learners and to overcome the obstacles that trainees perceive in implementing new behaviors. The following best practices guide the use of discussions during training sessions:

- For discussion activities, vary group sizes. Discussions can be conducted among the whole group, small groups, or pairs of participants.
- Provide clear goals and direction for discussions. For example, are participants

to answer specific questions, generate solutions or ideas, or complete another task? Provide a handout that details discussions' tasks and expected outcomes.

- Specify the amount of time for the discussions.
- Describe the rules the group should use to conduct discussions. For example, should discussions be brainstorming sessions in which all answers are considered, or should participants exercise judgment about the suggestions they offer in discussions?
- Plan time to wrap up the results of discussion before moving on to the next section of the training. During the wrap-up, reinforce the major themes that emerged from discussions. Acknowledge creative ideas and conflicting results. Be sure to explain how discussions met the learning objectives of the session. Did they introduce a topic or help to identify content, skills, processes, procedures, or best practices for trainees? Do not assume that trainees will automatically make the connection between discussions and the goals of the training session.

A nearly unlimited number of learning activities can be integrated into a training session. Excellent works can be found that describe training activities, some general and some specific to early childhood education.

Apply the best practices described here in your lectures, activities, demonstrations, and discussions. Let's look at how they can be applied to the introduction and body of a session on family-style meal service.

Example
. . . .

Topic: Family-Style Meal Service

Introduction
- Introduce trainer; participants introduce themselves.
- Ice-breaker: food-service relay race
- Overview of learning objectives
- Group discussion of family-style meal service experiences and accreditation criteria (activate prior experience and learners' need to know)

Body of the Session
Part 1: Overview of benefits to children and families of family-style meal service (general-to-specific design)

- Small-group discussion: merits of family-style meal service
- Large-group discussion: obstacles to conducting family-style meal service

Part 2: Process and procedure for introducing and using family-style meal service (procedural design)

- Demonstration: family-style meal service procedures
- Role play: conducting a family-style meal

Spotlight on Training Resources

Resources to support the development of training activities and games can be found through a number of sources. As you develop your training repertoire, collect activity and game ideas for future use. Consider developing a file system to collect, organize, and store your ideas. Organized resources will speed up development of your training by providing examples on which new instructional designs can be based.

Many of the training resources available commercially are not devoted specifically for training early childhood professionals. Adapt the content to match the unique objectives of your training sessions.

Internet

The Internet offers a wealth of resources for trainers. Use search terms such as "training games" and "employee training" to identify Web sites with ideas for trainers. Some resources can be downloaded for free; others require fees for use.

Library

Your local library is likely to have at least a few books with training ideas. Community libraries may have fewer of these resources; academic libraries such as those found at community colleges or universities are likely to have a broader selection. Training resources are usually located in the business section alongside other books on human resources.

Booksellers

Books on training activities and games are available at bookstores.. Some books focus on topics like ice-breakers or closers. Others present a wider range of training activities and games that you can adapt to your training topic. Books that focus on training are often found in the business section with other books on human resources, like hiring or coaching. Two books that focus specifically on early childhood education are Margie Carter and Deb Curtis's *Training Teachers: A Harvest of Theory and Practice* and Nancy P. Alexander's *Early Childhood Workshops that Work! The Essential Guide to Successful Training and Workshops.*

When you select activities from resources, use the same caution about infringing on copyright as you would in considering the purchase of prepared training materials. The checklist presented in chapter 6 on page 83 can help you make wise choices.

Before finalizing the content of a training session, two additional considerations merit attention: the plan for transferring of training to on-the-job behavior and the opportunity for assessing the learning that occurred in the training.

Planning for Practice and Transfer of Learning

At the beginning of this book, we proposed that the primary goal of training is to change on-the-job behavior. Therefore, it makes good sense that the design and development of the training session ensure that what is learned in the training session can actually be applied in the workplace. Trainers refer to "transfer of learning" or "training transfer" as the application of what is introduced and practiced in training to the actual environment in which the trainees work.

Some experts estimate that as little as 30 percent of what is learned in training is actually applied on the job (Broad 2005, 1). While there are many reasons for this unfortunate statistic, trainers can clearly do a lot to improve the results of their training efforts and to increase the application of training in the classroom. While you are developing the content and activities for the training session, consider the following tools to increase learning during training.

Examples

Using concrete examples during the training session's lectures, discussions, demonstrations, and activities increases trainees' ability to apply what they have learned. It is a best practice among trainers to use the examples uncovered during your assessment and analysis. For example, imagine you observed a teacher using a very effective sing-along technique during one of your training observations. Later, you conduct a training session with the goal of increasing the use of music among classroom teachers. The sing-along technique you observed could be presented as an example to demonstrate one practice that trainees could adopt. Examples make the content real, approachable, and specific.

Organizers, Handouts, and Job Aids

Providing trainees with materials to help them apply the skills and knowledge they practiced in training can greatly enhance their classroom performance. Handouts or job aids that review key steps in processes or procedures or that review the essential elements of the training are especially effective. For more information on job aids, see the spotlight section on page 115.

Memory Devices

Common sense tells us that teachers are more likely to use the information from their training if it is easy to remember. Trainers use a variety of memory devices to help trainees remember the training information. Three of the most common memory devices are acronyms, numbering, and alliteration.

Acronyms are abbreviations made up of first letters of several important words. For example, the acronym ADDIE stands for Analysis, Design, Development, Implementation, and Evaluation. Using this acronym makes it easier to remember each of the steps in the instructional design process.

Numbered lists are another commonly used memory device. For example, trainers might present Three Features of a New Program or Five Steps to Guidance Success. Numbered lists not only help organize content into smaller chunks; they also provide a mental model that most adults can remember.

Finally, alliteration, or the repetition of initial consonants, is a memory device often used in training. For example, in the next chapter we will introduce the four P's of successful training presentations. In this case, we have combined a numbered list with alliteration for the purpose of making the elements—prepare, practice, prompt, and praise during training preparation—easy to remember.

Practice

We all know the saying "practice makes perfect." Nothing beats practice for enhancing the development of skills and knowledge introduced during trainings. Practice opportunities in training sessions can be organized as simulations, role play, games, or drills. Practicing helps trainees remember important content and perfect the techniques associated with skills. Well-constructed practice activities can increase trainees' incentive to try new ideas in the workplace.

Commitment to Act

One of the most overlooked ways to improve the transfer of learning to the job is also the simplest. Often trainers fail to tell trainees that they are expected to use the information or skills presented in the training on the job. Trainers may assume that trainees will automatically adopt new techniques or that the training has made it clear that a change of behavior is expected. In reality, most adults expect explicit instruction about how, when, how often, and by whom new practices should be used.

In addition to stating explicitly that changes in performance are expected, trainers can enhance trainees' commitment to act by giving them a chance to plan for action as part of the training session. Planning for action or change is usually included just before or during the session's closing. As a best practice, trainers set aside time for trainees to commit in writing to how they will incorporate the information and skills from the training session into their teaching practices. A simple Action Plan example follows. For a reproducible copy, see form 19 in the appendix.

Action Plan

· ·

Training session title _____

Name _____

Date of action plan _____

In the spaces that follow, write three things covered in today's training session that you plan to incorporate into your teaching practice. Also write the time line for your plan and any support you will need to act on these new ideas.

CHANGE New idea or change in teaching practice from training session	TIMING Time line—when will you begin and when will change occur?	SUPPORT What support do you need in fulfilling your action plan?
1.		
2.		
3.		

Each of these techniques—examples, organizers, memory devices, practice, and commitment to act—can be included in the training session to enhance the transfer of training to classroom practice. In addition, trainers can plan for several activities *after* the training session that can enhance training transfer. Three of the most common supports for training transfer are reminders, coaching and feedback, and managerial support. Although each of these techniques is used after the training session, its use should be planned in advance of the training session.

Reminders

Classroom teachers are busy and have little time for contemplation or reflection. As they return to their busy lives in the classroom, they can easily set aside the new ideas introduced in training. Although they may have good intentions to pick up these ideas again when time allows, they often need helpful reminders.

Reminders can take several forms. One common reminder used by trainers is sending a follow-up note or postcard to trainees reminding them of the commitments they made during training. Using the dates from the trainees' action plans can enhance the value of reminders. Sending a reminder just before one of the action plan's due dates is a great way to spur a trainee to action.

Coaching and Feedback

Most change in on-the-job performance takes some time to perfect and to become part of day-to-day teaching routines. Regular coaching and feedback are extremely helpful, perhaps essential, in order to achieve a real and lasting change in behavior. Trainees often try new skills on the job for a period of time and then slip back into old habits, allowing the new ideas to diminish or disappear. Positive reinforcement such as coaching and feedback can remind teachers to continue using their new skills. Coaching and feedback can also encourage them to incorporate their new skills if they have not yet done so.

If you train and supervise teachers in a program, the plan for coaching and feedback following training will be relatively easy to accomplish. Simply create a schedule of observations during which you will have ample opportunity to provide coaching and feedback. Your attention to this task also reminds teachers that you consider this change in performance important.

In the event that you do not supervise the teachers for whom you are providing training, you can still help support coaching and feedback following training sessions. Two best practices are often used to do this. The first is to provide a checklist for the supervisor to use when observing trainees following the training session. The checklist does not have to be long or complex to be effective. Providing even a short, three- to five-item checklist reminds the supervisor to look for new behaviors among the trainees and signals the importance of coaching and feedback in reinforcing the use of the skills from the training session.

A second best practice is to ask trainees to provide coaching and feedback to one another. Organizing pairs of trainees who will support one another in the workplace can be a very effective way to get commitment to try new skills, create motivation, and ensure coaching and feedback after the training session. A checklist can be a helpful tool for trainees to use with their peers. When introducing this technique in your training session, allow time in the agenda for pairs to discuss how and when observing or coaching can take place. It may also be helpful to discuss a few simple ground rules to use when observing, coaching, and providing feedback to peers.

Managerial Support

The support of management is critical in transferring of training to on-the-job behavior. When teachers feel support from managers, their motivation to practice and master new skills is enhanced. Conversely, when teachers feel that their manager does not support the use of the knowledge or skills from the training session, they are unlikely to integrate these skills into their teaching practices.

If you are the manager or supervisor of the teachers for whom you provide training, showing your support for changes in their performance will be relatively easy. You can express your support during the opening and closing of the training session. You can also provide rewards or incentives for teachers who embrace ideas from the training session. The rewards do not have to be expensive to be effective; even inexpensive certificates of accomplishment or other small tokens signal to teachers that you have noticed their efforts. Public recognition at a meeting or at the next training event is also a good way to demonstrate your support for teachers who learn new skills or apply new knowledge.

You can still affect managerial support even when you are not the supervisor or manager of your trainees. In some cases, you can encourage managerial involvement in the training session. This is especially important in instances when a great deal of change is expected from the trainees. Consider asking the manager to introduce you and the topic in the opening portion of the training. This signals to the teachers that you have the endorsement of the manager and that she is supportive of the ideas you will be introducing. Another helpful technique is to develop a follow-up and reinforcement plan with the manager prior to conducting the training session. Whenever possible, provide the manager with all the materials needed to implement the plan. This helps ensure that the support and follow-up will be conducted as planned.

Spotlight on Job Aids

Job aids serve an important function by extending the training session into the workplace. Job aids can be used in a variety of situations; although they are not always introduced in training sessions, they are often used as a part of the plan for transfer of training to performance on the job. Job aids are those items that you expect trainees to continue to use on the job as reminders of specific information.

You probably already have a number of job aids in your work environment even if the term *job aid* is new to you. For example, you may have a short list of frequently used phone numbers by your telephone or an emergency evacuation map posted in each classroom. These are both job aids.

Developing high-quality job aids that will positively affect performance requires some planning and practice. The following principles can help guide you in the development of job aids:

- Keep them simple. Job aids are used during work. They should be used and understood at a glance. Overly complex job aids will be discarded quickly or will distract attention from the work at hand.
- Use visuals, graphics, or flowcharts when possible. Illustrations can simplify job aids and increase their value to trainees.
- Be selective. Create job aids only for those situations in which they can truly enhance performance. Too many job aids will create confusion and diminish the chances that they will be used.
- Apply job aids to situations in which details matter. Job aids match best with situations that are specific and detail-oriented. Use job aids for recipes, procedures, and directions that are challenging to remember and must be implemented accurately.
- Use a clear, straightforward design. Select simple fonts such as Ariel or Times New Roman. Avoid overuse of clip art and fancy fonts. Remember, you want to promote at-a-glance use.
- Build them to last. Because job aids will be used on the job, they need to be durable. Paper job aids should be made from heavyweight papers such as cardstock and laminated to extend their life.
- Date them. Procedures and policies change from time to time. Always date any new job aids with a month and year. You will be able to easily identify outdated job aids and replace them with new, up-to-date versions.

Assessing Learning and Checking for Mastery

Malena thought about the training session she conducted yesterday. She wondered how many of the teachers really learned the new procedures introduced in the training: "They seemed to like the training, but it is hard to tell how much they will remember today."

The goal of any training session is to change the trainees' on-the-job behavior. That goal is only met when trainees have successfully mastered the knowledge and skills introduced and practiced during the training session. When trainees have fulfilled the learning objectives constructed for the session, they are more likely to continue to practice their newfound knowledge and skills on the job and make them part of their regular teaching practice.

One of the important responsibilities the trainer assumes is assessing what the trainees learned. Trainers use many of the same techniques that teachers use to assess the learning of children in their classroom: observation, activities, and assessment tests. More about assessment of learning is found in chapter 9. For now, you will need to plan time in your sessions to assess your trainees' learning.

Closing

The closing is the final part of the training you should develop. Much like the opening and body of the training session, the closing should contain specific goals. Trainers often believe they can improvise a closing for the training based on what happened during the training session. While the events of the session will definitely affect your closing, you should have a plan for the closing in mind before the session. Remember, this is your final chance to leave a lasting impression on your trainees. You want to end your session with a strong statement.

The closing portion of the training session usually includes the following elements:

- time for action planning and commitment to transfer of training
- review of the learning objectives and acknowledgment that each has been addressed during the session
- final call for questions or clarification on any of the areas discussed or introduced
- time to complete session evaluations or assessments of learning
- acknowledgment of the trainees' participation and cooperation (a thank-you to the trainees)
- recognition of any supporting players, such as managers or training site organizers

Develop a Closing for the Session

Topic _____

Details of training session (if known)

Date _____ Time _____

Location _____

General description of content to be addressed _____

_____

_____

Create a short outline of the closing for your training session. Use this checklist to ensure that you have included the essential elements in your closing.

☐ Action planning
☐ Review of learning objectives
☐ Final questions
☐ Evaluations
☐ Acknowledgments
☐ Documentation

Brief overview of the closing _____

_____

_____

_____

_____

_____

_____

- distribution of training certificates or any other documentation needed by the trainees as evidence of their participation in the session

Use the form on page 117 to develop the closing for your training session. The checklist will help you to be certain you have included all of the important elements. For a reproducible copy of Develop a Closing for the Session, see form 20 in the appendix.

Putting It Together

Now it is time to pull your ideas for the opening, body, and closing of the training session together into one cohesive outline. As you do so, you will want to look at the materials in this book to check for some of the basic principles associated with a well-rounded training session. This is also the time to organize all the pieces that must be constructed to support the training session and to check the timing of the session. You may need to eliminate materials or adjust activities to fit the available time. Look at the plan for a training session on family-style meal service that follows. Notice that the activities, training materials (handouts, training aids, job aids), and estimated timing for each piece of the session are described.

As you review this plan, look for the same things you might look for in a well-constructed experience for children. For example, you should be looking for

- a balance of active participation and times when trainees are less active.
- a balance of instructor-led and participant-led activities.
- a balance of individual, small-group, and whole-group activities.
- opportunities to meet each of the learning objectives fully.
- opportunities for the trainer to observe and assess the learning of the trainees during discussion or activity.
- opportunities for practice of skills and application of knowledge.
- use of trainees' prior experiences and knowledge.

You can see each of these elements in the design example. You can also see attention to training transfer and the use of adult learning principles. Using these same ideas and elements, you can develop an outline for a training session you are planning. For a reproducible copy of Development Outline, see form 21 in the appendix.

Before you implement your training session, you will need to fully construct your training materials and completely develop your outline. Trainers have their own preferences about how scripted training materials should be. You may feel comfortable training using a well-developed outline like the provided example. Others may prefer that each section be completely described. In general, it is preferable to have the introduction or opening and the closing fully developed, even scripted. The body of the

Example

Topic: Family-Style Meal Service

SECTION	DESCRIPTION	MATERIALS	TIMING
Introduction	• Introduce trainer; participants introduce themselves • Ice-breaker: food-service relay race Divide participants into four teams. Each team must collect one of each food service tool. Participants race one at a time through mini obstacle course, answer a question, and receive a service tool. First team with a complete set wins. • Overview of learning objectives (presentation by trainer) • Group discussion of past experiences with family-style meal service • Accreditation criteria related to family-style meal service (presentation by trainer)	• Props for food-service relay: cups, spoons, ladles, etc. • Chart: learning objectives • Chart: accreditation criteria • Handout: accreditation criteria	30 minutes
Body, Part 1	• Merits of family-style meal service—small-group activity Divide participants into four groups. Assign each group one domain of development. Ask groups to generate ideas about how development in this domain is enhanced by children's participation in family-style meal service. Groups create chart and report to larger group. • Obstacles to conducting family-style meal service Large-group discussion facilitated by trainer. Generate list of obstacles. Ask participants to generate solutions to address each obstacle.	• Training aid: domains described on index cards, one for each small group • Chart paper	30 minutes
Body, Part 2	• Demonstration of family-style meal service by trainer with volunteers • Role-play family-style meal service Divide into four teams; role-play meal service taking turns in the role of the teacher. • Discussion—what did we learn from the role play, additional obstacles and benefits	• Handout: family-style meal service tips • Meal service utensils: enough for demonstrations and four role-play groups	30 minutes
Closing	• Action plan Individually complete action plan; share with a partner for support and to gain commitment to act • Review learning objectives Presentation by trainer, obtain agreement from trainees that learning objectives were met • Discuss final questions • Complete survey of trainees • Acknowledge participation and site support • Distribute training certificates	• Handout: action plan • Chart: learning objectives • Handout: survey of trainees • Training certificates	30 minutes

Development Outline

. . . .

Topic _____

Objectives

1. _____

2. _____

3. _____

SECTION	DESCRIPTION	MATERIALS	TIMING
Introduction			
Body			
Body			
Closing			

training should be carefully outlined with enough detail to remind you about timing and the materials you will need for each section. If the content is new to you or the topic is extremely technical, consider a more scripted approach. If you are very familiar with the topic, you may only need a detailed outline and a few scripted notes.

Most training material is designed and developed for specific implementation—that is, for a particular group of teachers, perhaps on a particular day. The implementation of the training materials you have designed and developed is the opportunity for all of the hard work you have invested to begin to pay dividends for your program. For most trainers, the actual training session is the most energizing part of the training task. The interactions, challenges, and rewards that come from helping other people master a new skill or discover some new piece of knowledge are often what entice trainers to continue training.

Many trainers develop their own styles. Ultimately, most trainers adapt their training techniques and style to fit the learning objective, design of the training, and audience. Many best practices guide the presentation of training materials to adult learners. These best practices are addressed in the next chapter.

Summary

Instructional design using the ADDIE model is a step-by-step process in which trainers analyze, design, develop, implement, and evaluate training materials. Although this process is widely used by trainers, trainers must make many choices to address the learning objectives they have defined while designing the training.

In developing the opening, body, and closing of a training session, trainers use many of the same best practices that are familiar to classroom teachers. They observe and assess to understand the needs of learners and they evaluate the effectiveness of their instruction. They use instructor- and participant-led learning activities. They balance individual, small-, and large-group activities. Finally, trainers plan for the transfer of learning to on-the-job practice. This important step ensures that learning objectives will be met and the behavior of participants will change to meet expectations.

CHAPTER 8 Implementing Training

Marcella stared at her notes. Her throat was dry and her palms were clammy. She thought to herself, "Why did I agree to train at this conference? My life was already stressful enough. Too late to cancel—the session starts in ten minutes. Well, here goes nothing!"

Lights, camera, action! When the time comes to implement the training you have constructed, the show finally begins. While presenting the actual training session is the most enjoyable aspect of the job for most trainers, being center stage can also be nerve-racking. We already discussed the importance of understanding your audience in the steps for designing and developing training sessions using the ADDIE model. The *I* in the ADDIE model— implementation of the training session—is the time to put this knowledge to work.

Many resources exist to support development of presentation and facilitation

skills. Some trainers attend train-the-trainer courses to support their development of presentation skills. These approaches can be helpful to your development as a trainer, but most trainers will also tell you that the most helpful developmental activity is practice. As with most skills, training improves you as a trainer. With practice, you will learn how to prepare, anticipate obstacles, and adapt to whatever presents itself during training sessions.

As you hone your skills as a trainer, keep in mind the four P's of successful training presentations: prepare, practice, prompt, and praise. Using these four behaviors will greatly increase your chances of presentation success.

Prepare

Experienced trainers have developed a variety of techniques to help them prepare for delivery of training. These include techniques for managing nervousness and the pitfalls that come with leadership responsibilities. Still, most trainers will tell you that they never completely eliminate nervousness or a few pre-training jitters. In fact, the energy that comes from nervousness is stimulating for most trainers and helps propel them to higher levels of success.

An unprepared trainer may occasionally fool a group of trainees with her charisma and quick thinking, but over the long run, preparation—or lack of it—shows. Three kinds of preparation are required for any training session: preparation of the materials, preparation of the trainer, and preparation of the environment (Vaughn 2005, 191–209).

First, prepare your materials. Besides constructing the basic training session, prepare all the handouts, training aids, and visuals that you will use to conduct the session. Most trainers estimate that up to three hours of preparation is required for each hour of training conducted. Use the checklist on page 125 to help you make sure you have completely prepared your materials. For a reproducible copy of Training Materials Checklist, see form 22 in the appendix.

Second, you must prepare yourself. As the leader of the session, you play a crucial role in its success. Your credibility can enhance or undermine the training's content. Although we should not judge a book by its cover, in fact we often select books based on appearance. For the same reason,

do not overlook your appearance while preparing your training session. The following best practices will help you present a credible cover:

- Dress one step above the level of dress you expect from the trainees. If you think most of the trainees will be dressed business casual, plan to wear traditional business attire.
- Limit your accessories. While simple jewelry can enhance an outfit and give a pulled-together look, too much can distract your trainees. Be careful about jewelry that makes noise as you move. Jangling bracelets or necklaces can be particularly distracting. Two or three simple accessories should be your limit.
- Plan for a polished look. Be sure clothes are neat and pressed. Your appearance signals your level of preparation.
- Dress comfortably, if not casually. Be sure that you are comfortable. Layers will help you adjust to the training room's temperature.
- Wear comfortable shoes. Remember that you will be on your feet before, through, and after the session.
- Wear something that makes you feel good. An outfit you like or that you know suits you can be a confidence booster.
- Get a good night's sleep before the training session. Eat a light meal an hour or so before the training session, and bring a bottle or two of water so you can stay hydrated.

Training Materials Checklist

· ·

Topic _____

Date _____

Check each of the following boxes to ensure that you have completely prepared the content and materials for the training session.

☐ Content has been thoroughly reviewed.

☐ Handouts have been created and reviewed, including spelling.

☐ Training aids and props have been gathered.

☐ Directions for games and activities have been reviewed and checked for accuracy.

☐ Visuals have been created, including PowerPoint slides, charts, video, etc. Spelling has been checked on all visuals.

☐ Specifics about trainees have been reviewed.

☐ Introduction has been memorized.

Spotlight on Team Training

Some trainers enjoy training in pairs or small teams. Novice trainers can often gain confidence from training with others. When training with others, keep a few best practices in mind:

- Training with another person requires *extra* preparation. Not only will you need to prepare the session itself, you will also need to prepare the interactions between the trainers so the session is organized and cohesive.
- Be certain that all of the trainers agree on the session's outline, timing, and objectives.
- Prepare well in advance. Team training frequently involves negotiating with others. Leave time for the adjustments than must be made to create a cohesive session.
- Practice the session together. The only way to truly understand how well the pieces of a team session fit together is to practice. A practice session allows you to polish the transitions between trainers and to understand the way each trainer works.

Pascal studied the training room with quiet determination. He looked up and addressed the event organizer. "Aren't we expecting fifty people for this session? I only see thirty chairs." The organizer quickly left to find the additional chairs in another room. "Wow, I'm glad I came early," thought Pascal. "That could have been a disaster!"

Third, prepare the training environment. It has a strong impact on the success of a training session. The following checklist includes the environment factors most critical to success. Using it can help you avert costly errors and last-minute confusion during your training sessions. For a reproducible copy of Training Environment Checklist, see form 23 in the appendix.

Plan ahead for typical obstacles. For example, it is wise to bring extra bulbs for projectors and an extension cord in case battery-operated devices are not charged. Unexpected occurrences will pop up from

Training Environment Checklist

Topic _____

Date _____

Location _____

Check each of the boxes as you prepare the environment for your training session.

☐ Training room is organized as requested (e.g., seating, tables, etc.).

☐ Training aids are available as requested (e.g., easel, podium, screen, etc.).

☐ Audiovisual (AV) equipment is available and in working order (e.g., microphones, LCD projectors, overhead projector, etc.). All equipment has been tested.

☐ Lighting is appropriate and adjustable if needed for AV. Controls have been located and directions for use verified.

☐ Refreshments for meals or breaks are scheduled and confirmed.

☐ Name tags or name cards are available for participants.

☐ Fresh markers for flipcharts or write-on boards are available.

time to time. When they do, remain calm, focus on adaptations, and use your sense of humor. Trainees are typically extremely forgiving, especially if they can see that you are otherwise well-prepared.

Practice

Absolutely nothing beats practice for improving training skills and presentation techniques. It can increase your level of comfort with the content and improve how you explain activities, clarify objectives, and articulate steps in processes and procedures.

Practice is extremely helpful in enhancing basic presentation skills. During practice, in addition to monitoring content, play close attention to these aspects:

Eye Contact

Make regular eye contact with your trainees, but don't engage them in a staring match. If you are using notes, look up regularly. In fact, you should be glancing at notes only occasionally and making eye contact with participants most of the time.

Tone of Voice

Be careful that your pitch is comfortable and that you are loud enough to be heard by participants without shouting. When people are nervous, the tone of their voice often rises.

Gestures

Use natural, unobtrusive gestures. A few simple gestures near the midpoint of your body help to accentuate points you are making. Big or startling gestures distract from your message.

Speed and Pacing

When we are nervous, we speak rapidly. Because many trainers feel rushed to cover a great deal of content in a short amount of time, they tend to speed up their delivery. The results can be incomprehensible to trainees. They are often hearing the information you are covering for the first time, so slow your speech to a normal conversational rate. Hint: if you are feeling out of breath, you are certainly talking too fast!

Enthusiasm

It is important to win the full attention of your trainees. Your enthusiasm about a topic will go a long way toward creating interest and motivation during your session. Smile; your attitude will be contagious.

There are many ways to practice. Some trainers practice training sessions by themselves in front of a mirror. Others use videotape or audio recording to check tone of voice, rate of speech, content, and delivery. You may also choose to practice in front of others and get a critique of your performance. If you do, select people who will give you honest feedback and help you improve your skills. While negative feedback is challenging to hear, it can help you be more successful as a trainer in the long run.

Trainers use a number of best practices to manage nervousness and to reduce its negative effects:

- Drink room-temperature water. Room-temperature water has the best effect on vocal chords and the throat. Avoid caffeinated beverages immediately before and during training sessions. Caffeine increases the effects of nervousness, especially dry mouth.
- Before training begins, close your eyes and envision yourself conducting the session successfully. Seeing the success in your mind is relaxing and provides confidence.
- Slow your rate of breathing. Taking a few deep breathes in and out can be extremely relaxing.
- Arrive at the training site early. Nothing heightens nervousness or creates stress more than feeling rushed. Treat yourself to an early arrival so you have plenty of time to check the room, your visuals, and every piece of equipment.
- Over-prepare your opening or introduction. Usually you will be most nervous at the start. Once things get rolling, nervousness subsides.
- Stretch and relax your muscles. A few quick stretches can help you relax and eliminate that feeling of tenseness that comes with nerves. Reach out to your sides, then reach to the sky, stretching through your shoulders and back. Tighten and release your arm and leg muscles.

Remember, your trainees have attended the training session to learn. They have not come to pass judgment or with the assumption that the experience will be negative. Your trainees want you to succeed because they also want to succeed. You and your trainees are in it together!

Prompt

You can prompt participation and success. You have already planned for many of these factors in your training design. Incorporating interactive experiences and planning for individual, small, and whole group activities will help enhance your trainees' participation. In addition to these design elements, use these best practices for prompting involvement and interaction:

- Make connections with trainees by greeting them as they arrive.
- Be visible and available during breaks to answer questions. This practice reminds trainees that you are interested in their success.

- Ask open-ended questions. Open-ended questions signal to trainees that you want to hear from them and that you value their contributions.
- Be mindful of the body language and facial expressions of trainees. Watch for indications that trainees are overwhelmed or need further clarification of important points.

Another way to prompt the success of your trainees is to refine two of the most challenging points in typical training sessions: introducing and concluding training activities. Training sessions often become derailed before or after activities because of unclear directions. Carefully prepare the directions you will use when introducing activities. Test the directions on someone who is unfamiliar with the activity. After introducing an activity, observe the trainees' behavior to be sure they are responding as you expected. Do not hesitate to provide additional direction if the activity is not starting out as planned. Redirecting the group is preferable to wasting valuable training time.

Take the same amount of care you took in setting up an activity when you conclude it. Reserve a few minutes of time to be sure that participants made the connection you intended between the activity and the learning objectives. This is also a great time for a short group discussion using open-ended questions. This technique helps you make a connection to the learning objectives and allows you to test what your trainees have learned. You can also use this time to answer any questions raised by the activity. Consider one or two of the following questions to prompt interaction at the conclusion of an activity:

- What did you learn from this activity?
- Why do you think this activity is important to our topic?
- What insights did you gain from participating in this activity?
- How does this activity relate to our learning objectives today?

Praise

Adult learners appreciate knowing that they are successful. Providing praise to your trainees serves several important goals. It encourages continued participation and enhances motivation and readiness to learn. Not all praise has a positive effect on the training session. The following best practices should inform your use of praise.

Be Specific

Give praise that describes specific contributions. "That's a creative idea" or "You have reached a thoughtful conclusion" provide examples of the behavior you want to see repeated.

Avoid Hollow Praise

If you praise everything, your praise quickly becomes meaningless. Use your comments strategically to identify the best ideas and the most meaningful contributions. Unlike children, adults can usually tell when you are not sincere in your praise. Do not run the risk of insulting trainees with insincere praise.

Encourage Further Contributions

Praise can help reluctant participants risk contributing more, for example, "You have the beginning of a great idea there; tell me more about what you are thinking."

Keep Everyone Together

Praise can be used to discourage a contributor who is monopolizing the conversion or getting ahead of the group. For example, "Nita, you are so far ahead of us; hold that thought for a minute while we explore a few ideas and catch up to you." This type of response acknowledges the trainee's understanding of the topic while keeping the training on track.

Using praise carefully throughout your session motivates your trainees and you. It is fun and energizing to recognize that your trainees are learning and successful. Have fun with this aspect of your role as the trainer. The more you are enjoying the session, the more likely your trainees will enjoy it.

Enhancing Training Skills

Over time, you will become increasingly comfortable with all aspects of your role as a trainer. Like any new set of skills, training becomes easier with practice and experience. You can enhance your training skills using a number of best practices:

- Read and pay attention to the feedback of your trainees. If you watch your results over time, you will see that you are improving in a variety of areas. You may also be able to target one or two areas that require further attention and development.
- Watch veteran trainers whom you admire. Continuing to learn from others is a great way to enhance your own skills. Watching experienced trainers address challenging participants or adjust to unexpected events can add new skills to your repertoire.
- Keep notes about your experiences. Use a journal or logbook to keep notes about your experiences. Note what went well and what areas need some enhancement. Use these notes to develop your skills.
- Solicit the opinions of trusted experts. Ask those you trust to observe your training and provide feedback on your performance. Although it is not always easy to hear criticism, it is extremely useful in improving your training skills.

One of the most important tools a trainer possesses is an open mind. Continuing to learn will help you be effective in supporting the learning of others. Learning will also help you enjoy your role as a trainer more deeply and feel the pride that comes with success.

Summary

Support your careful planning of a training session with excellent facilitation and presentation. Preparation and performance engage learners and create results that trainees can use on the job.

The four P's of training implementation—preparation, practice, prompt, and praise—combine to create an effective delivery of training material. Trainers who prepare thoroughly and practice repeatedly are more likely to overcome nervousness and deliver solid training content. Similarly, trainers who use prompts to develop connections with trainees and praise their efforts judiciously enhance participation and learning.

Trainers are also learners. Trainers who continue to be students of their own work will grow in their effectiveness and pleasure in the trainer role.

CHAPTER 9 Training Evaluation

Hadley smiled as the trainees left the room. "So many compliments," she said to her mentor. "I guess they really learned a lot." Her mentor smiled back at her and quietly said, "They certainly enjoyed themselves. But how do you know they really learned about your topic?"

The final step in the instructional design process is evaluation. Although it is the last step, it is one of the most important. Evaluation tells the trainer about the success of her training session. Evaluation also provides information that can help her improve her performance and strengthen the next training session she offers.

Evaluation has a number of purposes and can be conducted with a variety of tools. Although it is usually conducted after a session, the evaluation should be planned beforehand.

Training is usually evaluated using one or more of four levels. These are reaction, learning, behavior, and results. Nearly all training evaluations use the reactions of the trainees. This is considered level 1 evaluation. Level 2 evaluation (learning) is also relatively common because most trainers are extremely interested in how well their trainees learned the content of the training. Levels 3 and 4 (behavior and results) are rarely evaluated. These levels represent the most important aspect of the training session's success because they measure the extent to which training content is applied on the job.

Level 1 Evaluation: Reaction

The most common form of training evaluation is measuring participant reaction. Nearly all formal training sessions include some kind of survey or other feedback device to gather trainees' reactions. These tools are often referred to as smile sheets

Spotlight on Donald Kirkpatrick

The four levels of training evaluation are often referred to as Kirkpatrick's Four Levels of Evaluation. This is because the design of this model of training evaluation is credited to Donald Kirkpatrick.

Donald Kirkpatrick has been active in the training profession since the 1950s. His approach to training evaluation was first introduced to the profession through a series of articles for the American Society for Training and Development (ASTD) in the late 1950s and early 1960s. Since then, Kirkpatrick's Four Levels have become the most well-known and widely used framework for evaluating training. Donald Kirkpatrick is professor emeritus at the University of Wisconsin and has been bestowed almost every award available in the training profession, including ASTD's highest award, the Lifetime Achievement in Workplace Learning and Performance.

In recent years, other professionals have extended Kirkpatrick's model or proposed revisions based on their own work. Most trainers continue to use all or some of the Kirkpatrick model as the basis for their approach to training evaluation.

and sometimes are undervalued by trainers. While it is easy to dismiss the reactions of participants as uninformed opinions, these nonetheless represent the views of the customers or consumers of the training session and can tell the trainer a great deal about the likelihood that skills or knowledge from the training will be applied on the job. The trainer also can learn about what skills and development needs she needs to pay attention to by the reactions of participants (Kirkpatrick and Kirkpatrick 2006, 21–22).

To develop such an evaluation tool, first determine what you want to measure. You must know what you want your trainees'

reaction to be in order to ask the correct questions. For example, if you cannot change the time of day during which training is offered, do not ask trainees to react to this aspect of the training. Most reaction questionnaires or surveys include questions about

- the level of difficulty or challenge of the training content.
- the extent to which the content applies to the trainees' work.
- the organization of the content.
- the trainer's preparation and presentation.

Some reaction questionnaires also ask about the logistics of the training—location, time, room arrangements, food, and so on. Gathering information about the logistics can help you plan future training sessions, especially if these arrangements can be changed.

Reaction questionnaires usually contain both open-ended questions and multiple-choice questions. The latter are much less time-consuming to tabulate. The answers to open-ended questions often provide richer detail and a wider range of information. Using a combination of these two types of questions provides you with the best results. The goals in developing your reaction form are to receive

- honest responses.
- responses from all of the trainees.
- feedback to help you develop as a trainer.
- feedback to help enhance future training events.
- feedback to suggest the level of support needed in transferring the training content to the workplace.

You can choose to use the same reaction questionnaire or survey for a variety of training sessions or create a new form for each training session. There are merits to each of these approaches. By using the same form each time, you can compare scores over time and measure your improvement as a trainer. You can also reach some reliable conclusions about adaptations you have made to training sessions. If scores are generally improving over time, you are on the right track. If scores are not improving or are declining, you may not have made the proper adjustments to content or approach.

Using a reaction questionnaire constructed specifically for each new training session allows you to completely customize your approach. You can ask questions that are specific to the content or to the audience. For example, you might ask about the trainees' reaction to a particularly complex part of the training or to an area in which trainees are known to be sensitive to change.

Most trainers develop a group of questions that they ask in each evaluation. The following sample survey has a number of general questions that can be used in a wide variety of training situations. A questionnaire similar to the example provided can be used again and again. For a reproducible copy of Training Survey: Level 1 Evaluation, see form 24 in the appendix.

Most reaction surveys do not include this many questions. You should carefully choose the questions you present. Remember that the evaluation is usually the last part of the training session; trainees may be eager to complete the session, and time is often running short. Whenever possible, limit your reaction survey to one side of a piece of paper. Always try to collect reaction information immediately. Allowing trainees to take reaction surveys with

Training Survey: Level 1 Evaluation

Thank you for your participation in the training session. Your candid responses to the following questions will help me to evaluate the success of this training session and improve future offerings.

Topics _____

Date _____ Trainer _____

Check the box that best describes your reaction to each statement.

S = Strongly Agree   **A** = Agree   **N** = Neutral   **D** = Disagree   **SD** = Strongly Disagree

	S	A	N	D	SD
THE SESSION CONTENT					
The material addressed in this session was relevant to my job.					
I found the material addressed in this session easy to understand.					
The material presented in this session was at the right level of challenge for me.					
I will use at least some of the information from this session in my work.					
THE PRESENTATION					
The trainer appeared to be well-prepared for the session.					
The presentation captured my interest.					
The trainer made the objectives of the session clear to me.					
I felt involved in the training session.					
My questions were answered in a manner that advanced my understanding.					

	S	A	N	D	SD
THE PRESENTATION (*continued*)					
The audiovisual material used by the trainer assisted in my understanding of the topic.					
The handouts distributed by the trainer were helpful to me as a learner.					
The trainer's style of delivery was a good match with my learning needs.					
THE TRAINING ENVIRONMENT					
The facilities were comfortable for me as learner.					
The training session seemed to last about the right amount of time.					
The training session was scheduled at a time of day that met my needs.					
I was able to locate the training session easily.					
Registering for the training session was easy.					

What was your overall impression of this training session? _____

_____

What was the best part of this session? _____

_____

What could be improved in the future? _____

_____

What, if anything, remains unclear to you? _____

_____

What future training topics would you recommend? _____

_____

them to be returned later will dramatically decrease the data you can collect.

Level 2 Evaluation: Learning

Training is the appropriate intervention when employees lack skills or knowledge, so measuring how well the training fills that void seems obvious and necessary. Unfortunately many trainings are conducted with no specific plans in place to evaluate whether or not trainees learned the content. Measuring learning should be central to evaluating the success of the training session.

Unlike reaction, learning requires evaluation from someone other than the trainees themselves. While you can certainly ask trainees what they learned during a session, their responses are imperfect measures of learning. Sometimes trainees may be reluctant to admit what they did not know prior to a training session, so their evaluation of what they learned may be underestimated. Sometime trainees will greatly overestimate what they learned in training to please the trainer.

Luckily, trainers have a number of techniques at their disposal that can help them more accurately evaluate the learning of their trainees. Many of these techniques will sound very familiar to you—they are often used by teachers to assess children's learning in the classroom.

Observation

One of the best ways to evaluate trainees' learning is by observing their participation in discussion activities during the training session. Including activities that require trainees' involvement allows trainers to stand back and observe. When trainers spend a great deal of the training session lecturing or presenting information, they have difficulty assessing trainees' learning.

Activities

Experienced trainers plan activities that provide an opportunity to assess the learning of the participants. This is why you often find simulation or role-play activities near the end of training sessions. These activities provide rich opportunities to assess trainees' ability to use new information. Applying information in a role play or simulation activity is an excellent demonstration of learning. Other activities that can be used to evaluate learning include question-and-answer, game show-style activities. These are often extremely fun for participants and provide great opportunities for you to assess their learning. You need to be aware of your dual role in facilitating the activity and assessing learning during these complex and sometimes demanding activities.

Tests or Quizzes

Some trainers use test or quizzes to evaluate the learning of the participants. Tests are often used in situations in which mastery of the information is essential. For example, most first aid courses require a test to demonstrate mastery of this highly detailed information.

Tests are often used in training sessions that support certifications or other credentials. Again, first aid courses or CPR training sessions are good examples of the skills for which use of tests is needed to evaluate learning and to support certification of trainees.

Finally, tests can create documentation of trainees' learning. Sometimes it is important to document the content mastered by trainees. In some regulatory situations, learning must be documented by more than attendance. Carefully constructed tests or quizzes can be used and retained as records of the trainees' participation and measures of the learning accomplished during the training session.

Quizzes or tests to document learning are based on the learning objectives. Multiple-choice, true-or-false, short-answer, or fill-in-the-blank questions can be used. When constructing the test or quiz, be certain that during the course of the training session you have completely addressed the content that will be evaluated. Never attempt to trick adult learners with obscure questions. This creates a lack of trust. Remember, your goal is for all of your trainees to master the content you present. If you have done your job well, all of your trainees should get perfect scores on the evaluation quiz!

Level 3 Evaluation: Behavior

Behavioral evaluation measures the extent to which trainees use the training content on the job. Why it is necessary to measure both learning and behavior? You may think that if trainees have learned the content, they will use it in the workplace. Unfortunately this is not always the case.

Sometimes training transfer is hindered because of forces outside the control of the trainees. For example, if trainees attend a training session on literacy and return to a classroom in which there are no books from which to read aloud, then it is unlikely that their behavior on the job will reflect their learning during the training session. Besides resources, training transfer can be influenced by peers, managers, and the trainee's level of confidence in using what was learned during the training session.

On-the-job behavior can be evaluated using a number of best practices. Obviously there are instances in which you won't be able to measure the behavior of trainees following training. For example, if you provide training as part of a conference or professional organization meeting, you may not have any further involvement with trainees. This is one of the reasons why this level of evaluation is conducted less frequently than reaction or learning. If you supervise the teachers for whom you conduct training or you have continuing involvement with their program, you should consider evaluations of behavior following training as essential. This level of evaluation measures the true effectiveness of the training and enhances your credibility as a trainer who gets results. Evaluations of trainee behavior are usually conducted using questionnaires or observations.

Questionnaires

One simple way to measure trainees' use of the training skills and knowledge is to ask *after* they have had a chance to apply what they have learned. Questionnaires are often used this way. The following questionnaire is an example of a tool you can use to measure trainees' self-assessment. For a reproducible copy of Training Survey: Level 3 Evaluation, see form 25 in the appendix.

Self-disclosures of behavior changes are imperfect. Trainees may underestimate their application of the skills and knowledge from training, or they may overestimate what they have accomplished. Although imperfect, trainee questionnaires to evaluate behavior are often the only or the most practical approach to evaluation at this level.

Observation

Observing trainees on the job is the best way to evaluate changes in behavior. If an observation was conducted as part of the analysis phase of the instructional design, the trainer can easily compare the behavior of trainees before and after the training session. Such an evaluation provides the strongest possible measure of behavior change.

Because observations can be time-consuming, many trainers observe only a sampling of the trainees. A few trainees are observed before and after the training to understand the potential for change among the entire group of trainees. If behavior change is evident in the sample, it can be extrapolated to all or most of the trainees.

Often the post-training observations will be conducted by the trainees' supervisor or manager. If the supervisor is someone other than the trainer, you will need to create a plan and obtain agreement so that the observations reflect your expectations, as explained during the training session. This consistency demonstrates managerial support for transfer of training.

Most trainers use a checklist to conduct observations of trainees' behavior. If post-training observations are planned, share the checklist that will be used with the trainees. This technique reinforces the expectation that on-the-job behaviors among trainees must change following the training session. Observation checklists can be constructed by the participants as job aids; these are often provided just before the close of the training session.

Training Survey: Level 3 Evaluation

· ·

Topic _____

The purpose of this questionnaire is to determine the extent to which you have had the opportunity to use the information presented in last month's training session. Your candid response will help us support your training needs and improve our training programs.

Check the box that best describes your use of the training content.

GE = Great Extent, **SE** = Some Extent, **L** = Little, **N** = Not at all

	GE	SE	L	N
I have been able to apply what I learned in the training in the classroom.				
My manager has supported my use of the skills I learned in the session.				
My peers have supported my use of the skills I learned in the session.				
The skills introduced in the training session met my needs in the classroom.				
I was able to use the skills and knowledge from the training session with little adaptation.				
I feel comfortable using the skills I learned in the training session as part of my teaching practice.				

What aspects of the training have been easy to apply in the classroom? _____

_____

What has been challenging to apply? Why? _____

_____

What obstacles have hindered your ability to apply what you learned in the training session?

_____

What additional support do you require to apply all that you have learned? _____

_____

Level 4 Evaluation: Results

··

Loretta reviewed the report from her licensing agent and glowed with pride. Her program had struggled in recent inspections but passed with flying colors this time. She said to herself, "All that training has really paid off. Not one single violation for hand washing or any of the food service rules. What a difference!"

Results, the final level of evaluation, measure the extent to which the training session has changed the results of the organization. This level of training evaluation is very valuable for the organization and the trainer. Nevertheless, it is rarely conducted because it requires thoughtful and time-consuming planning before and after the training session.

Measures of training results help explain why training is valuable for the program and support the continued expenses of providing training. For example, if a trainer is able to show that a training session on classroom safety resulted in 10 percent fewer employee accidents over the course of a year, the value of the reduced workers' compensation claims and accident-related absences would more than pay for the cost of the training session. But to support such a statement, the trainer would need information from a period of time before and after the training was conducted. The trainer would also need to calculate the average expenses

of accidents in order to determine the savings. Finally, the trainer would need to know the cost of the training. This information helps the trainer determine whether the value of the results exceeded the expense of the training. Although this is challenging information to gather, it is very valuable to the organization conducting the training session.

Training results can be related to a wide variety of organizational factors. Commonly measured training results include

- reductions in accidents.
- reductions in absences.
- reductions in employee and child turnover.
- increases in customer satisfaction.
- increases in new enrollment.

Not all results affect a program financially. You may choose to measure results that do not offset the cost of the training but are valuable to the organization, such as achieving accreditation or a higher level in a quality rating system. Other types of nonfinancial results that can be measured include

- test or assessment scores among children in the program.
- quality rating scores such as the Early Childhood Environment Rating Scale (ECERS) or the Infant/Toddler Environment Rating Scale (ITERS).
- improved licensing status.

- ability to participate in state-sponsored or agency-sponsored programs.
- awards or other recognition such as employer of choice awards.

Evaluating results requires collecting data before and after training sessions. It also requires patience. Most results of this type do not occur overnight or even within a few weeks or months. Many results can only be tracked over the course of a year or more. Before beginning an evaluation at this level, you must be sure the organization is interested in a long-term evaluation project. Be selective about which training programs you attempt to evaluate at this level. Only training programs that require considerable investment typically merit evaluation efforts of this kind.

Training evaluation is the final step in the ADDIE instructional design process. As you have probably guessed, the results of your evaluations will provide many ideas for adapting and improving your training designs and development. That is why many trainers think of the ADDIE model as a circle in which evaluation provides inspirations for additional analysis, design, development, and so on.

Summary

Trainers, like classroom teachers, must understand and evaluate their work. Evaluation establishes the results of the training session and helps the trainer to improve her skills over time.

Trainers use the four levels of evaluation developed by Kirkpatrick to understand the reactions, learning, behavior, and results of trainees. Each level of evaluation has a distinct purpose and assesses a different aspect of the training's results. A variety of techniques are used to evaluate training at each of these levels. Evaluation techniques include questionnaires, observations, and tests or quizzes. These evaluations can provide a robust understanding of the effectiveness of the training session in changing teacher behavior on the job, which is the ultimate goal of training.

References

Albrecht, Kay. 2002. *The right fit: Recruiting, selecting, and orienting staff.* Lake Forest, IL: New Horizons.

Brandon, Richard N., and Ivelisse M. Martinez-Beck. 2006. Estimating the size and characteristics of the United States early care and education workforce. In *Critical issues in early childhood professional development*, eds. Martha Zaslow and Ivelisse M. Martinez-Beck, 49–76. Baltimore: Paul H. Brookes.

Bredekamp, Sue, and Carol Copple, eds. 1997. *Developmentally appropriate practice in early childhood programs.* Rev. ed. Washington, DC: National Association for the Education of Young Children.

Brinkerhoff, Robert O. 2006. *Telling training's story: Evaluation made simple, credible, and effective.* San Francisco: Berrett-Koehler.

Broad, Mary L. 2005. *Beyond transfer of training: Engaging systems to improve performance.* San Francisco: Wiley.

Clark, Ruth C., and Chopeta Lyons. 2004. *Graphics for learning: Proven guidelines for planning, designing, and evaluating visuals in training materials.* San Francisco: Pfeiffer.

Dittmann, Melissa. 2005. Generational differences at work. *Monitor on Psychology* 36 (6): 54–55.

Fukkink, Ruben G., and Anna Lont. 2007. Does training matter? A meta-analysis and review of caregiver training studies. *Early Childhood Research Quarterly* 22 (3): 294–311.

Galagan, Pat. 2006. Engaging generation Y: An interview with Marcus Buckingham. *Training & Development* 60 (8): 27–30.

Gilbert, Thomas F. 2007. *Human competence: Engineering worthy performance.* Tribute ed. San Francisco: Wiley.

Kagan, Sharon L., Kristie Kauerz, and Kate Tarrant. 2008. *The early care and education teaching workforce at the fulcrum: An agenda for reform.* New York: Teachers College Press.

Katz, Lilian G. 1995. *Talks with teachers of young children.* Norwood, NJ: Ablex.

Kirkpatrick, Donald L., and James D. Kirkpatrick. 2006. *Evaluating training programs: The four levels.* 3rd ed. San Francisco: Berrett-Koehler.

Knowles, Malcolm S. 1980. *The modern practice of adult education: From pedagogy to andragogy.* Chicago: Follett.

Lancaster, Lynne, and David Stillman. 2007. *Bringing out the best in every generation: Performance beyond ClashPoints*. Washington DC: BridgeWorks.

Loo, Tristan. 2006. Success coaching: Create SMART goals. Marlboro, NJ: Self Improvement Inc. http://www.selfgrowth.com.

Maxwell, Kelly L., Cathie C. Feild, and Richard M. Clifford. 2006. Defining and measuring professional development in early childhood research. In *Critical issues in early childhood professional development*, eds. Martha Zaslow and Ivelisse M. Martinez-Beck, 22–48. Baltimore: Paul H. Brookes.

National Association for the Education of Young Children. 2005. *NAEYC early childhood program standards and accreditation criteria: The mark of quality in early childhood education*. Washington, DC: National Association for the Education of Young Children.

National Research Council. 2001. *Eager to learn: Educating our preschoolers*. Washington, DC: National Academy Press.

Taylor, Kathleen, Catherine Marienau, and Morris Fiddler. 2000. *Developing adult learners: Strategies for teachers and trainers*. San Francisco: Jossey-Bass.

Tout, Kathryn, Martha Zaslow, and Daniel Berry. 2006. Quality and qualifications: Links between professional development and quality in early care and education settings. In *Critical issues in early childhood professional development*, eds. Martha Zaslow and Ivelisse M. Martinez-Beck, 77–110. Baltimore: Paul H. Brookes.

Vaughn, Robert H. 2005. *The professional trainer: A comprehensive guide to planning, delivering, and evaluating training programs*. 2nd ed. San Francisco: Berrett-Koehler.

Appendix

1 Training Plan: Compliance Training

Program name _____

What agencies govern the program? _____

_____

_____

What other programs, such as accreditation, quality rating systems, or special funding sources, affect the training requirements?

PROGRAM	IMPACT

Briefly list some of the training requirements with which the program must comply.

New employee orientation _____

_____

Annual training requirements _____

_____

Special topics (first aid, CPR, blood-borne pathogens, child abuse detection and reporting, shaken baby syndrome, food handling, medication administration). List each topic and the training requirements.

TOPIC	TRAINING REQUIREMENTS

2 Training Plan: Program Goals

Program name _____

Use the space below to draft two or three program goals that will affect your training plans in the next two or three months.

1. _____

   _____

   _____

   _____

   _____

2. _____

   _____

   _____

   _____

   _____

3. _____

   _____

   _____

   _____

   _____

Now, review each goal. Does it fit the SMART formula—is it Specific, Measurable, Attainable, Relevant, and Time sensitive? If not, revise your goals to incorporate each of these elements.

3 Trainer Self-Assessment

Name _____   Date _____

Check the box that best describes your abilities and attributes at this time.

PERSONAL ATTRIBUTES	Not at all	Somewhat	Mostly	Always
I am considered an effective communicator.				
I respect confidences and personal information.				
I am able to be fair in handling conflicts and disputes.				
I convey respect for others, including those with different perspectives from my own.				
I enjoy learning new things.				
I usually consider change to be positive.				
I am flexible and can adapt quickly to changing circumstances.				
SUBJECT MATTER KNOWLEDGE				
People often seek my input on concerns or problems related to the program.				
I regularly attend trainings or otherwise update my knowledge about early childhood education.				
I value diverse points of view about program goals, procedures, and outcomes.				
TRAINING METHODS				
I am comfortable in front of others.				
I can present information forcefully and clearly.				
I am a good listener.				
Others find me motivating.				
I am able to recognize anxiety or discomfort in others.				
I know and can use a wide variety of training techniques.				
I am interested in what others think and say about my training abilities.				
STRATEGY AND LEADERSHIP				
I am able to link program concerns or goals to training solutions.				
I am able to prioritize the needs of teachers.				
I often am selected to lead groups or projects.				
I am aware of a wide variety of resources available in my community.				

List each item to which you responded "not at all" or "somewhat." These are your areas to concentrate on when creating your professional development plan.

4 Putting Andragogy to Work

Topic or training idea _____

PRINCIPLE	IDEAS TO CONSIDER
The Learner's Need to Know	• •
The Learner's Self-Concept	• •
The Learner's Experiences	• •
The Learner's Readiness	• •
The Learner's Orientation to the Learning Task	• •
The Learner's Motivation	• •

5 Training Plan: Individual Teacher Profile

. . . .

Date _____

Teacher's name _____

Years of experience _____

Educational background _____

Generational influences _____

Stage of teacher development _____

Unique talents, interests, experiences, and characteristics _____

_____

_____

_____

_____

Unique challenges and needs _____

_____

_____

_____

Notes _____

_____

_____

_____

_____

_____

_____

_____

_____

6 Orientation Worksheet

For each aspect of the orientation, describe the materials that will be used and the way in which the information will be introduced.

Program philosophy, values, and goals	Materials _____ _____ Methods of introduction _____ _____
Expectations for ethical conduct	Materials _____ _____ Methods of introduction _____ _____
Health, safety, and emergency procedures	Materials _____ _____ Methods of introduction _____ _____
Individual needs of children in the classroom assignment	Materials _____ _____ Methods of introduction _____ _____
Accepted guidance and classroom management techniques	Materials _____ _____ Methods of introduction _____ _____
Daily activities and routines of the program	Materials _____ _____ Methods of introduction _____ _____

Adapted from *NAEYC Early Childhood Standards and Accreditation Criteria: The Mark of Quality in Early Childhood Education,* Standard 6, Criterion 6.A.03. Copyright © 2005 by the National Association for the Education of Young Children.

Program curriculum	Materials _____ _____ Methods of introduction _____ _____
Child abuse and neglect reporting procedures	Materials _____ _____ Methods of introduction _____ _____
Program polices and procedures	Materials _____ _____ Methods of introduction _____ _____
NAEYC Early Childhood Program Standards	Materials _____ _____ Methods of introduction _____ _____
Regulatory requirements	Materials _____ _____ Methods of introduction _____ _____
Follow-up training to expand on initial orientation	Materials _____ _____ Methods of introduction _____ _____

Adapted from *NAEYC Early Childhood Standards and Accreditation Criteria: The Mark of Quality in Early Childhood Education,* Standard 6, Criterion 6.A.03. Copyright © 2005 by the National Association for the Education of Young Children.

7 Observation: Group Time

Check the box that best describes the extent to which each behavior is observed.

1 = to a very little extent, **2** = to a little extent, **3** = to a great extent, **4** = to a very great extent

	1	2	3	4
Children are invited to the group time in an organized and thoughtful way.				
The group-time routine is familiar to the children; the children know what to expect.				
The group-time activities are appropriate to the children's level of development and interests.				
The group-time activities are presented in a way that is engaging to the children.				
The teacher's planning meets the needs of the children.				
The group time ends in a logical manner; it is clear to the children how to transition to the next activity.				

Comments _____

_____

_____

_____

_____

8 Training Survey

Teacher's name _____

I feel my strengths as a teacher include _____

_____

_____

_____

_____

Some of the areas I feel I can improve include _____

_____

_____

_____

_____

I would like additional information or training on the following topics _____

_____

_____

_____

_____

_____

_____

_____

_____

9 Training Survey: Sample Using Rating

Dear Teacher:

We are currently planning our training offerings for the upcoming year. In order to create plans that meet your individual needs, we are asking for your help in gathering information about your interests.

Rate your level of interest in receiving training on the topics listed below.

Teacher's name _____

S = Strongly Agree   **A** = Agree   **N** = Neutral   **D** = Disagree   **SD** = Strongly Disagree

I am interesting in training about:	S	A	N	D	SD
Child guidance techniques					
Classroom planning					
Literacy activities					
Math activities					
Classroom routines, such as meals					
Early childhood theory					
Other: _____					

10 Training Survey: Sample Using Ranking

Dear Teacher:

We are currently planning our training offerings for the upcoming year. In order to create plans that meet your individual needs, we are asking for your help in gathering information about your interests.

Rank your level of interest in receiving training on the topics listed below. Rank each item from 1 to 5, with 1 representing your highest priority and 5 your lowest priority. Use each number only once.

Teacher's name _____

Training topics	Rank
Classroom planning	
Conducting child assessment	
Planning for family conferences	
Planning for outdoor play	
Confronting challenging child behaviors	

11 Individual Professional Development Plan

Teacher's name _____

Compliance training required _____

_____

Results of training needs assessment—areas of interest, needs, and current challenges
to be addressed by training _____

_____

_____

Development Goal #1 _____

Training methods and activities   Deadline

1. _____   _____

2. _____   _____

3. _____   _____

4. _____   _____

Development Goal #2 _____

Training methods and activities   Deadline

1. _____   _____

2. _____   _____

3. _____   _____

4. _____   _____

Development Goal #3 _____

_____

Training methods and activities   Deadline

1. _____   _____

2. _____   _____

3. _____   _____

4. _____   _____

Development Goal #4 _____

_____

Training methods and activities   Deadline

1. _____   _____

2. _____   _____

3. _____   _____

4. _____   _____

12   Evaluating Training Materials for Purchase

Answer each question by circling YES or NO. Carefully consider any items that you mark NO.

Do the objectives of the materials match your program's needs?	YES	NO
Do the activities and examples fit the program?	YES	NO
Can the materials be used with very little adaptation?	YES	NO
Can the materials be copied to meet your needs?	YES	NO
Is the source of the material credible?	YES	NO
Is the material of a quality you will be proud to use?	YES	NO
Can any parts of the training materials that do not meet your needs be eliminated?	YES	NO
Are the materials easy to read, logically ordered, and sufficiently detailed?	YES	NO
Does the cost of the materials fit within your budget?	YES	NO
Is the expense of the training materials a good value?	YES	NO

13 Training Survey: Family-Style Meal Service

The topic for our teacher training session next month will be Family-Style Meal Service. We have identified this practice as an opportunity to enhance our program and to move closer to meeting accreditation criteria. Please complete the following questionnaire to help us create the training session that will best meet your needs and facilitate a smooth transition to this new practice.

Please circle the response that best matches your point of view. Write any additional comments in the space provided.

YES   NO   I am familiar with the concepts underlying the use of family-style meal service.

YES   NO   I am using or have used family-style meal service in my classroom.
If YES, how would you describe those experiences?

_____

_____

_____

YES   NO   I am excited about the idea of trying family-style meal service in my classroom.
Please explain why or why not.

_____

_____

_____

What challenges, if any, do you anticipate as we implement family-style meal service?

_____

_____

_____

Thank you for your thoughtful contributions!

14   Change Management Questionnaire

1. How great is the difference between the desired behavior and the current behavior? How much do teachers need to change their on-the-job behaviors or routines to be consistent with the training session's objectives?

2. Which teachers, if any, are already using the desired skills or behaviors? Will these teachers be willing to speak on behalf of the desired or new behaviors during the training sessions? Are the teachers using the desired behaviors considered leaders among the group?

3. Are some parts of the content more challenging than others? Can the more challenging parts of the content be introduced after the more agreeable content has been addressed and the group is working productively?

4. How do the teachers in this group respond to changes in ways of doing things? Are most open to change in general? Is change infrequent or frequent? Have changes in the past been implemented smoothly or only with significant challenges?

5. What are the possible challenges that teachers face when implementing the new behaviors or skills introduced in the training? Are these challenges manageable? Are the solutions to the challenges within the teachers' control?

6. What are the benefits of implementing new ideas, skills, or behaviors to teachers? What are the benefits to children? Do changes make the teachers' days more manageable or enjoyable?

7. If you have worked with this group of trainees before, in what ways do they usually resist change? Are they vocal about their misgivings? Do they challenge new ideas immediately or wait until the trainer solicits feedback?

15 Training Session Planner

Topic _____

Details of training session (if known)

Date _____ Time _____

Location _____

General description of content to be addressed

_____

_____

Change management considerations

_____

_____

Training audience—who, experience, diversity, special needs

_____

_____

Training environment—where will training take place, furnishings, equipment, etc.

_____

_____

Special considerations (if any)

_____

_____

_____

16   Identifying Objectives

Topic _____

Details of training session (if known)

Date _____   Time _____

Location _____

Write a general description of content to be addressed.

_____

_____

_____

_____

Create two or three learning objectives for your training session. Remember, your learning objectives should answer the questions who? what? when? and how well?

1. _____

_____

_____

_____

2. _____

_____

_____

3. _____

_____

_____

17 Webbing a Training Topic

Topic _____

Identify the central idea of the training topic in the middle circle. Then identify a few subtopics related to the central idea and some of the smaller ideas related to each subtopic. Use the session's learning objectives to guide the development of your topics. Add additional circles to the web as needed to capture the content for the training session.

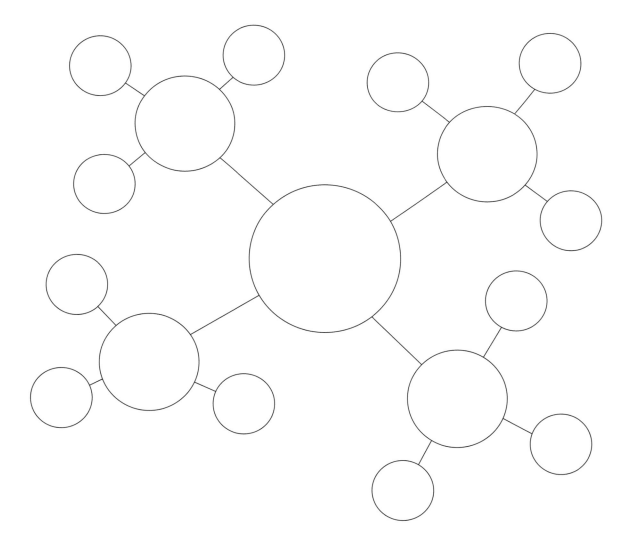

18 Develop Your Introduction

Topic _____

Details of training session (if known)

Date _____   Time _____

Location _____

General description of content to be addressed _____

_____

_____

Develop a plan for the introduction to your training session. Use the following short checklist to ensure that you have addressed all of the important elements found in an introduction.

☐ Attention-getting opener
☐ Trainer's introduction
☐ Overview of agenda and logistics details
☐ Ice-breaker or team-builder (if appropriate)
☐ Explanation of the learning objectives and trainees' need to know

Brief overview of the introduction _____

_____

_____

_____

_____

_____

_____

_____

19   Action Plan

Training session title _____

Name _____

Date of action plan _____

In the spaces that follow, write three things covered in today's training session that you plan to incorporate into your teaching practice. Also write the time line for your plan and any support you will need to act on these new ideas.

CHANGE New idea or change in teaching practice from training session	TIMING Time line—when will you begin and when will change occur?	SUPPORT What support do you need in fulfilling your action plan?
1.		
2.		
3.		

20　Develop a Closing for the Session

Topic _____

Details of training session (if known)

Date _____　　Time _____

Location _____

General description of content to be addressed _____

_____

_____

Create a short outline of the closing for your training session. Use this checklist to ensure that you have included the essential elements in your closing.

- ☐ Action planning
- ☐ Review of learning objectives
- ☐ Final questions
- ☐ Evaluations
- ☐ Acknowledgments
- ☐ Documentation

Brief overview of the closing _____

_____

_____

_____

_____

_____

_____

_____

_____

21 Development Outline

Topic _____

Objectives

1. _____

2. _____

3. _____

SECTION	DESCRIPTION	MATERIALS	TIMING
Introduction			
Body			
Body			
Closing			

22 Training Materials Checklist

. . . .

Topic _____

Date _____

Check each of the following boxes to ensure that you have completely prepared the content and materials for the training session.

- ☐ Content has been thoroughly reviewed.

- ☐ Handouts have been created and reviewed, including spelling.

- ☐ Training aids and props have been gathered.

- ☐ Directions for games and activities have been reviewed and checked for accuracy.

- ☐ Visuals have been created, including PowerPoint slides, charts, video, etc. Spelling has been checked on all visuals.

- ☐ Specifics about trainees have been reviewed.

- ☐ Introduction has been memorized.

23 Training Environment Checklist

Topic _____

Date _____

Location _____

Check each of the boxes as you prepare the environment for your training session.

☐ Training room is organized as requested (e.g., seating, tables, etc.).

☐ Training aids are available as requested (e.g., easel, podium, screen, etc.).

☐ Audiovisual (AV) equipment is available and in working order (e.g., microphones, LCD projectors, overhead projector, etc.). All equipment has been tested.

☐ Lighting is appropriate and adjustable if needed for AV. Controls have been located and directions for use verified.

☐ Refreshments for meals or breaks are scheduled and confirmed.

☐ Name tags or name cards are available for participants.

☐ Fresh markers for flipcharts or write-on boards are available.

24 Training Survey: Level 1 Evaluation

Thank you for your participation in the training session. Your candid responses to the following questions will help me to evaluate the success of this training session and improve future offerings.

Topics _____

Date _____ Trainer _____

Check the box that best describes your reaction to each statement.

S = Strongly Agree   **A** = Agree   **N** = Neutral   **D** = Disagree   **SD** = Strongly Disagree

	S	A	N	D	SD
THE SESSION CONTENT					
The material addressed in this session was relevant to my job.					
I found the material addressed in this session easy to understand.					
The material presented in this session was at the right level of challenge for me.					
I will use at least some of the information from this session in my work.					
THE PRESENTATION					
The trainer appeared to be well-prepared for the session.					
The presentation captured my interest.					
The trainer made the objectives of the session clear to me.					
I felt involved in the training session.					
My questions were answered in a manner that advanced my understanding.					

	S	A	N	D	SD
THE PRESENTATION (*continued*)					
The audiovisual material used by the trainer assisted in my understanding of the topic.					
The handouts distributed by the trainer were helpful to me as a learner.					
The trainer's style of delivery was a good match with my learning needs.					
THE TRAINING ENVIRONMENT					
The facilities were comfortable for me as learner.					
The training session seemed to last about the right amount of time.					
The training session was scheduled at a time of day that met my needs.					
I was able to locate the training session easily.					
Registering for the training session was easy.					

What was your overall impression of this training session? _____

_____

What was the best part of this session? _____

_____

What could be improved in the future? _____

_____

What, if anything, remains unclear to you? _____

_____

What future training topics would you recommend? _____

_____

25 Training Survey: Level 3 Evaluation

Topic _____

The purpose of this questionnaire is to determine the extent to which you have had the opportunity to use the information presented in last month's training session. Your candid response will help us support your training needs and improve our training programs.

Check the box that best describes your use of the training content.

GE = Great Extent, **SE** = Some Extent, **L** = Little, **N** = Not at all

	GE	SE	L	N
I have been able to apply what I learned in the training in the classroom.				
My manager has supported my use of the skills I learned in the session.				
My peers have supported my use of the skills I learned in the session.				
The skills introduced in the training session met my needs in the classroom.				
I was able to use the skills and knowledge from the training session with little adaptation.				
I feel comfortable using the skills I learned in the training session as part of my teaching practice.				

What aspects of the training have been easy to apply in the classroom? _____

_____

What has been challenging to apply? Why? _____

_____

What obstacles have hindered your ability to apply what you learned in the training session?

_____

What additional support do you require to apply all that you have learned? _____

_____